Think Big, Act Bold: A Mindset Makeover for Women Entrepreneurs

D0836489

Megan Ewing

To my loving husband, who has always encouraged me to chase my dreams and supported me through every twist and turn of this wild entrepreneurial journey. To my beautiful children, who remind me every day that anything is possible with a little imagination and a lot of hard work. And to my amazing parents, who instilled in me the values of perseverance, resilience, and always striving for excellence. Without all of you, this book would not have been possible. Thank you for being my constant source of love and inspiration.

CONTENTS

INTRODUCTION

Welcome to Think Big, Act Bold: A Mindset Makeover for Women Entrepreneurs! This book is dedicated to all the women out there who are pursuing their dreams and building businesses that make a difference in the world. Whether you're just starting out on your entrepreneurial journey or you're a seasoned business owner looking to take your business to the next level, this book is for you.

Let's start by looking at the current state of women entrepreneurship. Despite making up almost half of the workforce, women are still underrepresented in entrepreneurship. In the United States, for example, women-owned businesses account for just 42% of all businesses, and they tend to be smaller and less profitable than male-owned businesses.

While we are still underrepresented in entrepreneurship we are growing and we are making a huge difference. Just imagine what these statistics are going to be in a few years as we continue to work on our own dreams and passions.

Women entrepreneurs also face unique challenges, such as access to funding, gender bias, and work-life balance. However, the potential benefits of women entrepreneurship are significant, including job creation, economic growth, and social impact.

As a woman entrepreneur myself, I know firsthand the challenges and obstacles that we face on our journey to success. From navigating the male-dominated business world to overcoming self-doubt and imposter syndrome, it can be tough to stay focused, motivated, and inspired.

That's why I wrote this book. I want to share with you the strategies, insights, and wisdom that I've gained over the years as an entrepreneur, author, and coach. My goal is to help you develop the mindset and habits that will empower you to achieve your goals, overcome challenges, and create a life and business that you love.

One thing I've learned on this journey is mindset is the key to success in any aspect of life. Whether it's getting in shape, building a business, raising children, or loving ourselves, everything starts with mindset.

In this book, we'll explore a wide range of topics related to mindset and entrepreneurship, including:

- Overcoming limiting beliefs and negative self-talk

- Building resilience and grace in the face of challenges

- Cultivating a strong sense of purpose and vision

- Developing essential habits and practices for productivity and focus

- Marketing and branding strategies for building a successful business

- And much more!

Throughout the book, you'll find practical tips, real-life examples, and exercises to help you apply the concepts to your own life and business. My hope is that this book will serve as a roadmap and a source of inspiration for you as you pursue your entrepreneurial dreams.

But let me be clear: this book is not a quick fix or a magic formula for success. Building a successful business and a fulfilling life takes hard work, dedication, and perseverance. It requires a growth mindset, a willingness to learn and grow, and a commitment to taking bold action in the face of uncertainty and risk.

That's why I've structured this book as a mindset makeover. We'll be exploring not only the practical strategies and tactics for building a successful business, but also the mindset and habits that will help you stay focused, motivated, and inspired on your journey.

So if you're ready to think big and act bold, if you're ready to unleash your full potential and create a life and business that you love, then let's dive in! Whether you read this book from cover to cover or dip in and out as needed, my hope is that it will empower you to achieve your dreams and create a better world for all of us.

CHAPTER 1: DREAMING BIG – WHY YOUR VISION MATTERS

Picture this: You're standing at the edge of a magnificent cliff overlooking a vast, glittering ocean. You can feel the warm sun on your face, the soft breeze tousling your hair, and the endless possibilities just waiting to be seized. You take a deep breath, spread your arms wide, and leap fearlessly into the unknown. Now, take that feeling of exhilaration, that boundless courage, and channel it into your entrepreneurial journey. That's the spirit of dreaming big.

Your vision is the foundation upon which your entire entrepreneurial empire will be built. It's the beacon that guides you, the fuel that propels you forward, and the compass that steers you in the right direction. In this chapter, we'll dive into why having a clear, ambitious vision is crucial for your success, and how you can expand your idea of what's possible.

Defining Your Dream Life and Business

Defining your dream life and business is a critical step in achieving success as a woman entrepreneur. It involves creating a clear vision of what you want to achieve and why, and then taking intentional actions to make that vision a reality.

Before you can start building your business, you need to know what you're building it for. What does your dream life look like? Are you traveling the world, speaking on stages, and inspiring millions? Are you creating a cozy, thriving family business that supports your loved ones? Or perhaps you're a trailblazer, breaking barriers and changing the world one innovation at a time.

To begin, take some time to reflect on your values, passions, and goals. What do you want your life to look like? What kind of business do you want to build? What impact do you want to make in the world? Write down your thoughts and ideas, and use them to create a vision statement that captures your aspirations and purpose.

Take some time to visualize your dream life in vivid detail. Imagine waking up every day excited to do what you love, surrounded by people who support and cherish you, and living in the kind of abundance that makes your heart sing. Write it all down and make it as specific as possible. This is your ultimate vision – the life you're working towards as you build your business.

Next, let's define your dream business. What are you passionate about? What unique gifts, talents, and experiences do you have to offer the world? Don't be afraid to think big here – remember, this is your dream. Consider the impact you want to have, the legacy you want to leave, and the difference you want to make.

Once you have a clear vision, you can begin to set specific, measurable, and achievable goals that will help you move closer to your dream life and business. Break down your goals into smaller, manageable steps, and create an action plan that outlines what you need to do to achieve each one. As you set your goals you can break them down even more and add your actionable items to your weekly or daily to-do list. This way you stay on track to accomplish your goals without getting distracted by things that come up in life.

It's important to stay flexible and adaptable as you work towards your goals. Be open to new ideas and feedback, and be willing to pivot and adjust your strategy as needed to stay on track. Don't be afraid to take risks and try new things, and be prepared to learn from both your successes and failures.

Remember, building a successful business and a fulfilling life takes time, effort, and perseverance. It's important to stay focused, motivated, and inspired on your journey, and to seek out the support and guidance you need to overcome challenges and achieve your goals. The best things in life don't come without work.

By defining your dream life and business, setting clear goals, and taking intentional action, you can create a life and business that you love and that makes a positive impact in the world. So go ahead, dream big, and take bold action to make your vision a reality.

The Importance of Having a Clear Vision

When you have a clear, compelling vision for your life and business, it's like having a high-powered rocket strapped to your back. It propels you forward, even when the going gets tough. It gives you a sense of purpose, a reason to keep pushing through obstacles and setbacks. Your vision is your "why," and when your "why" is strong enough, you'll find a way to make it happen.

Setting your "why" or your purpose is important in entrepreneurship because it gives you a clear direction and motivation for why you are building your business. Your "why" helps you define your goals, and serves as a guidepost for the decisions you make, the actions you take, and the people you surround yourself with. It gives you a reason to push through challenges and setbacks, and helps you stay true to your values and beliefs.

Moreover, having a clear sense of purpose and mission also helps you communicate the value of your business to others, including potential customers, investors, and partners. It allows you to connect with your audience on a deeper level and differentiate your business from competitors.

In summary, setting your "why" is a crucial step in building a successful and fulfilling entrepreneurial journey. It provides you with direction, motivation, and helps you stay true to your values and beliefs.
Having a clear vision is essential for achieving success as a woman entrepreneur. Your vision represents your aspirations, your purpose, and your ultimate goal for your business and your life. It provides a sense of direction and focus, and it guides your decisions and actions as you work towards your goals.

To create a clear vision, it's important to take the time to reflect on your values, passions, and goals. Consider what motivates you, what you want to achieve, and what kind of impact you want to make in the world. Write down your thoughts and ideas, and use them to craft a statement that captures your aspirations and purpose.

Your vision should be specific, inspiring, and realistic. It should be something that you are deeply committed to and that energizes and motivates you. It should also be achievable and aligned with your strengths, skills, and resources.

Once you have a clear vision, you can use it to guide your decisions and actions. Every choice you make should be evaluated against your vision, and if it doesn't align, it may not be the best choice for you and your business. By staying focused on your vision, you can avoid distractions and stay on track towards achieving your goals.

Additionally, having a clear vision can help you communicate your purpose and values to others, including potential customers, employees, and partners. It can serve as a rallying cry and inspire others to join you on your journey. One of the biggest mistakes entrepreneurs make is not understanding how to effectively communicate their purpose. With an employee position you are given a title and description, when you become an entrepreneur it's harder to explain exactly what you do for people to understand.

In summary, having a clear vision is critical for achieving success as a woman entrepreneur. It provides direction, focus, and motivation, and it guides your decisions and actions as you work towards your goals. By taking the time to define your vision and staying committed to it, you can create a business and a life that aligns with your values, passions, and aspirations.

A clear vision also helps you make better decisions. When you know where you're headed, you can ask yourself, "Will this choice bring me closer to my dream, or will it take me further away?" This clarity can save you countless hours, dollars, and heartaches on your entrepreneurial journey.

Expanding Your Idea of What's Possible

As women, we're often taught to play small, to be modest, and to not take up too much space. This can lead to us limiting our dreams, thinking we don't deserve greatness or that it's out of reach. But I'm here to tell you, gorgeous, that you are worthy of your wildest dreams, and you have the power to make them a reality. Let's take up space, play big, and show the world just how powerful us women are!

To expand your idea of what's possible, it's important to first identify and challenge the limiting beliefs that may be standing in your way. These beliefs may include thoughts like "I'm not good enough," "I don't have enough experience," or "I don't have the resources to succeed." By acknowledging these limiting beliefs and challenging them with positive affirmations and evidence to the contrary, you can begin to shift your mindset and open up new possibilities. Take some time to write down some of your personal limiting beliefs so that you can work on challenging them each day.

Surround yourself with people who dream big, too. Connect with other ambitious, successful entrepreneurs who inspire you to think bigger and push harder. I struggled with connecting with other entrepreneurs at first, most of my long time friends had an employee mindset and I valued the length of the relationships so long I didn't look for other relationships. As I began connecting with other entrepreneurs I started to feel more comfortable and more inspired. It was easier to connect because we were all going through similar things.

Read books, listen to podcasts, and attend events that stretch your mind and expand your horizons. Reading books has been life changing for me, I found confidence, self improvement, and amazing tips and advice that helped me achieve the success I have. Also, YouTube is an amazing resource for learning new things or educating yourself on topics that you are interested in.

It's also important to surround yourself with positive, supportive people who believe in you and your vision. Seek out mentors, peers, and advisors who can offer guidance and encouragement, and who can help you expand your perspective and see new opportunities.

Another key strategy for expanding your idea of what's possible is to embrace a mindset of abundance. Rather than focusing on scarcity and limitations, focus on the abundance of resources, opportunities, and possibilities that are available to you. By adopting this mindset, you can approach challenges with a sense of curiosity and creativity, and you can discover new ways to achieve your goals.

Another powerful tool to expand your idea of what's possible is visualization. Spend time each day imagining yourself living your dream life, running believe that your vision is possible and that you're capable of achieving it. If you are a visual learner, you can turn your visualizations into a vision board so you can see it on a regular basis. Place the vision board somewhere that you will see it everyday for a steady reminder.

Finally, it's important to take bold action and step outside of your comfort zone. This may mean trying new things, taking calculated risks, or pursuing opportunities that may seem daunting or unfamiliar. By pushing yourself to explore new possibilities and take on new challenges, you can expand your idea of what's possible and achieve greater success and fulfillment as a woman entrepreneur.

A fun way to do this is challenge yourself to try something that you may have considered just paying someone else to do. It may be some kind of graphic, a minor website edit, writing a blog post, whatever it is just challenge yourself to try something out of your comfort zone.

Conclusion

In this chapter, we've explored why having a clear, ambitious vision is crucial for your success as an entrepreneur. We've defined your dream life and business, and we've talked about the importance of surrounding yourself with people who inspire you to think big. We've also discussed the power of visualization and expanding your idea of what's possible.

Now, it's time to take action. Take the vision you've defined and start breaking it down into actionable steps. What can you do today, this week, and this month to move closer to your dream? How can you challenge yourself to think even bigger and aim even higher?

Remember, your vision is the foundation of your entrepreneurial journey. It's what will keep you going when things get tough, and it's what will guide you towards your ultimate destination. So dream big, gorgeous, and let your vision light the way!

"*Think like a queen. A queen is not afraid to fail. Failure is another stepping stone to greatness.*"
— *Oprah Winfrey*

CHAPTER 2: THE ENTREPRENEUR MINDSET – EMBRACING YOUR INNER BOSS

Welcome to Chapter 2 of Think Big, Act Bold! Now that you have a clear vision for your dream life and business, it's time to talk about the mindset you need to make it a reality. As an entrepreneur, your mindset is everything. It's what separates the successful from the struggling, the confident from the fearful, and the dreamers from the doers.

Embracing your inner boss means taking charge of your life and career, and not waiting for someone else to give you permission to pursue your dreams. It means recognizing your own potential and capabilities, and having the confidence to take risks and make decisions. Embracing your inner boss also means being comfortable with the idea of leadership and being able to inspire and motivate others towards a common goal. By cultivating this mindset, you can create a sense of empowerment and ownership over your life, and ultimately achieve success on your own terms.

In this chapter, we'll explore the mindset you need to cultivate in order to thrive as an entrepreneur. We'll talk about the importance of adopting a success mindset, overcoming the fear of failure, and the power of positive self-talk.

Cultivating a Success Mindset

Your mindset is the lens through which you view the world, and as an entrepreneur, it's important that your lens is focused on success. A success mindset is characterized by a deep belief in your ability to achieve your goals, a willingness to take risks, and a positive attitude.

Cultivating a success mindset is a critical step in achieving success as a woman entrepreneur. Not only is your mindset is the lens through which you view the world but also the mindset through which you view your own potential, and it can have a profound impact on your ability to achieve your goals.

A success mindset is one that is focused on growth, learning, and possibility. It involves cultivating a positive, optimistic outlook and embracing challenges as opportunities for growth and development. With a success mindset, you are able to bounce back from setbacks and failures, and you are able to stay motivated and focused on your goals even in the face of adversity.

So how do you cultivate a success mindset? Here are some key strategies to consider:

1. Practice gratitude. Gratitude is a powerful mindset that can help you stay positive and focused on what you have rather than what you lack. Take time each day to reflect on the things you are grateful for, and use that positive energy to fuel your actions and decisions.

2. Embrace failure. Failure is an inevitable part of the entrepreneurial journey, and it's important to view it as a valuable learning opportunity rather than a sign of weakness or defeat. By reframing failure as a stepping stone to success, you can develop greater resilience and perseverance.

3. Set ambitious goals. Setting ambitious goals can help you stretch yourself and achieve more than you ever thought possible. While it's important to set realistic goals, it's also important to challenge yourself and aim for big things.

4. Surround yourself with positive, supportive people. Your mindset is influenced by the people you spend time with, so it's important to surround yourself with positive, supportive people who believe in you and your vision. Seek out mentors, peers, and advisors who can offer guidance and encouragement, and who can help you stay focused on your goals.

5.   Practice self-care. Taking care of your physical, emotional, and mental well-being is essential for cultivating a success mindset. Make time for exercise, meditation, or other activities that help you stay centered and focused, and prioritize rest and relaxation to avoid burnout.

By cultivating a success mindset, you can develop the resilience, optimism, and focus necessary for achieving your goals as a woman entrepreneur. With the right mindset, you can overcome challenges, seize opportunities, and create a life and business that aligns with your values and aspirations.

Overcoming the Fear of Failure

Overcoming the fear of failure is a common challenge for many women entrepreneurs and also entrepreneurs in general. The fear of failure can be paralyzing, causing you to hesitate, second-guess yourself, or avoid taking risks altogether. However, failure is a natural and necessary part of the entrepreneurial journey, and learning how to overcome this fear is essential for achieving success.

One of the first steps in overcoming the fear of failure is to reframe your mindset. Instead of viewing failure as a negative outcome, try to view it as a valuable learning opportunity. Failure can provide insights into what went wrong, what you can do better, and what you need to change in order to achieve your goals. By embracing failure as an opportunity for growth and development, you can reduce your fear and anxiety and develop greater resilience and perseverance. Ask yourself, "What can I learn from this experience?" or "How can I use this setback to improve my business?"

Another strategy for overcoming the fear of failure is to break your goals down into smaller, manageable steps. Often, the fear of failure can arise when you are faced with a large, overwhelming goal that seems impossible to achieve. By breaking that goal down into smaller, more achievable steps, you can reduce your anxiety and build momentum towards your ultimate goal. Once your goals are broken down into smaller, manageable steps you can add these steps to your weekly or daily to-do list to help keep you on track for achieving the goals that you are setting.

It's also important to seek out support and guidance from mentors, peers, and advisors. These individuals can offer valuable insights, feedback, and encouragement, and can help you stay focused on your goals even in the face of setbacks and challenges. By surrounding yourself with positive, supportive people, you can build your confidence and reduce your fear of failure.

In addition, it's important to practice self-care and prioritize your well-being. The fear of failure can be emotionally and mentally draining, and it's important to take care of yourself in order to maintain your energy and focus. Make time for activities that help you relax and recharge, such as exercise, meditation, or spending time with loved ones.

Finally, it's important to remember that failure is not the end of the road. Even the most successful entrepreneurs have experienced failure, and it's often through those failures that they have learned the most and grown the most. By maintaining a growth mindset and viewing failure as an opportunity rather than a setback, you can overcome your fear of failure and achieve greater success and fulfillment as a woman entrepreneur.

In summary, overcoming the fear of failure is essential for achieving success as a woman entrepreneur. By reframing your mindset, breaking your goals down into smaller steps, seeking support and guidance, practicing self-care, and maintaining a growth mindset, you can reduce your fear and anxiety and develop the resilience and perseverance necessary for achieving your goals.

It's also helpful to remember that failure is temporary. Just because you fail at something doesn't mean you're a failure. It simply means you haven't found the right approach yet. Keep trying, keep learning, and eventually, you'll succeed.

The Power of Positive Self-Talk

The power of positive self-talk is a critical tool for women entrepreneurs who want to achieve success and overcome challenges. Self-talk is the internal dialogue that runs through your mind throughout the day, and it can have a profound impact on your mindset, confidence, and motivation. When you begin to focus on positive self-talk, if you are anything like me you will realize just how tough you are on yourself. We don't realize how much negative talk we say to ourselves that is having a negative impact on the value we give to ourselves.

Positive self-talk involves consciously replacing negative thoughts and beliefs with positive ones. By focusing on your strengths, accomplishments, and potential, you can cultivate a more optimistic and confident outlook, and build the resilience and determination necessary for achieving your goals.

One strategy for practicing positive self-talk is to use affirmations. Affirmations are positive statements that you repeat to yourself regularly, such as "I am capable," "I am worthy of success," or "I am making progress towards my goals." By repeating these statements throughout the day, you can reinforce positive beliefs and counteract negative self-talk. I encourage you to take some time and write down at least 10 affirmations to practice, these can be ones you made up or ones you found somewhere else.

Another strategy for practicing positive self-talk is to reframe negative thoughts and beliefs. For example, if you find yourself thinking "I'll never be able to do this," try reframing that thought as "I may not know how to do this yet, but I can learn and improve." By focusing on the potential for growth and improvement, you can shift your mindset from one of defeat to one of possibility.

It's also important to surround yourself with positive, supportive people who believe in you and your vision. Seek out mentors, peers, and advisors who can offer guidance and encouragement, and who can help you stay focused on your goals. By surrounding yourself with positive influences, you can reinforce positive self-talk and build your confidence and motivation.

Additionally, it's important to practice self-care and prioritize your well-being. Taking care of your physical, emotional, and mental health can help you maintain a positive mindset and stay motivated and focused on your goals. Make time for activities that help you relax and recharge, such as exercise, meditation, or spending time with loved ones.

In summary, the power of positive self-talk is a critical tool for women entrepreneurs who want to achieve success and overcome challenges. By using affirmations, reframing negative thoughts and beliefs, surrounding yourself with positive influences, and practicing self-care, you can cultivate a more optimistic and confident outlook, and build the resilience and determination necessary for achieving your goals.

Conclusion

In this chapter, we've explored the mindset you need to cultivate in order to thrive as an entrepreneur. We've talked about the importance of adopting a success mindset, overcoming the fear of failure, and the power of positive self-talk. Remember, your mindset is a key component of your success as an entrepreneur. By cultivating a success mindset, reframing your thinking around failure, and practicing positive self-talk, you can overcome obstacles and achieve your biggest goals.

Now, it's time to take action. Take a moment to reflect on your current mindset. Are there any negative thought patterns or limiting beliefs that are holding you back? How can you reframe those thoughts and adopt a more positive, success-oriented mindset?

As you go through your entrepreneurial journey, remember that your mindset will be constantly evolving. There will be ups and downs, successes and failures, but if you stay committed to cultivating a success mindset, you'll be able to weather any storm and come out on top.

In the next chapter, we'll dive deeper into the concept of limiting beliefs and how to break through them. Get ready to unleash your inner badass, gorgeous, because we're just getting started!

"*I never dreamed about success. I worked for it.*"
— *Estée Lauder*

CHAPTER 3: BREAKING THROUGH LIMITING BELIEFS

Welcome to Chapter 3 of Think Big, Act Bold! In this chapter, we'll explore one of the biggest obstacles to success for many entrepreneurs: limiting beliefs. Limiting beliefs are the stories we tell ourselves about what we can and can't do, what's possible and what's not. They're the invisible barriers that hold us back from achieving our biggest goals and living our best lives.

Some of these limited beliefs are beliefs that we may have inherited from our parents and other family members. Limiting beliefs from different generations can impact us without people realizing. We are in a different era in the world and some of the same worries and limiting beliefs just don't hold true today.

In this chapter, we'll identify the limiting beliefs that are holding you back, learn how to reframe and conquer them, and discover the freedom of living without self-imposed limitations.

Identifying Your Limiting Beliefs

Identifying your limiting beliefs is a critical step in achieving success as a woman entrepreneur. Limiting beliefs are deeply held assumptions and beliefs that you hold about yourself, your abilities, and the world around you, that can hold you back from achieving your goals.

Limiting beliefs can take many forms, such as "I'm not good enough," "I don't have enough experience," "I'm not smart enough," or "I'm not talented enough." These beliefs can be deeply ingrained and may stem from past experiences, societal expectations, or other factors.

To identify your limiting beliefs, it's important to start by becoming aware of your internal dialogue. Pay attention to the thoughts and beliefs that run through your mind throughout the day, especially those that are negative or self-critical. Journaling can be a helpful tool for tracking these thoughts and identifying patterns.

Once you have identified your limiting beliefs, it's important to challenge them with evidence to the contrary. For example, if you find yourself thinking "I'm not good enough to start a business," ask yourself why that thought is true, and look for evidence to the contrary. You might remind yourself of past accomplishments, positive feedback from others, or other factors that demonstrate your potential. Once you've identified your limiting beliefs, it's important to challenge them. Ask yourself, "Is this belief really true?" or "Where did this belief come from?" Often, our limiting beliefs are based on old, outdated stories that no longer serve us.

It's also important to seek out feedback from others, such as mentors, peers, or advisors. These individuals can offer an outside perspective and help you identify blind spots or areas where you may be holding yourself back. By seeking out feedback and constructive criticism, you can gain a more realistic view of your strengths and weaknesses, and develop a more accurate sense of your potential.

In addition, it's important to reframe your mindset and focus on growth and possibility. Instead of viewing your limitations as fixed and unchangeable, try to approach challenges with a growth mindset and a willingness to learn and improve. By embracing challenges as opportunities for growth and development, you can reduce the impact of your limiting beliefs and develop greater resilience and perseverance.

Finally, it's important to take action and step outside of your comfort zone. Often, limiting beliefs can be perpetuated by inaction or avoidance. By taking bold action and pursuing opportunities that may seem daunting or unfamiliar, you can challenge your limiting beliefs and build your confidence and resilience.

In summary, identifying your limiting beliefs is a critical step in achieving success as a woman entrepreneur. By becoming aware of your internal dialogue, challenging your limiting beliefs with evidence, seeking out feedback from others, reframing your mindset, and taking bold action, you can reduce the impact of your limiting beliefs and achieve greater success and fulfillment in your personal and professional life.

Reframing and Conquering Your Limiting Beliefs

The next step is to reframe and conquer your limiting beliefs. Start by replacing your limiting beliefs with positive affirmations. For example, if you believe that you're not good enough, replace that thought with, "I am capable and worthy of success." If you believe that success is reserved for other people, replace that thought with, "I am worthy of success and I will achieve it."

Reframing and conquering your limiting beliefs is an essential step in achieving success as a woman entrepreneur. Limiting beliefs can hold you back from reaching your full potential, but by reframing and conquering them, you can overcome self-doubt and achieve greater success.

Reframing your limiting beliefs involves challenging the negative thoughts and assumptions that hold you back. One technique for reframing is to ask yourself a series of questions to challenge your assumptions. For example, if you have the limiting belief that "I'm not good enough to succeed," you might ask yourself, "What evidence do I have to support this belief?" or "What would I say to a friend who had this belief?" By asking these questions, you can start to shift your mindset and challenge the negative assumptions that hold you back. By going through this process you can see where these limited thoughts may have come from and that will help with challenging them.

Another technique for reframing is to focus on the positive aspects of your situation. For example, if you have the limiting belief that "I don't have enough experience to start a business," you might reframe this belief as "I have a unique perspective and fresh ideas that can help me succeed." By focusing on your strengths and potential, you can shift your mindset and reduce the impact of your limiting beliefs. We are lucky to have so much information right at our fingertips so whatever experience we lack we can educate ourselves and change that.

Conquering your limiting beliefs involves taking action to overcome them. One way to do this is to break down your goals into smaller, more manageable steps. By taking small steps towards your goals, you can build momentum and confidence, and reduce the impact of your limiting beliefs.

Another way to conquer your limiting beliefs is to seek out support and guidance from mentors, peers, and advisors. These individuals can offer valuable insights, feedback, and encouragement, and can help you stay focused on your goals even in the face of setbacks and challenges. By surrounding yourself with positive, supportive people, you can build your confidence and reduce the impact of your limiting beliefs.

It's also important to practice self-care and prioritize your well-being. Limiting beliefs can be emotionally and mentally draining, and it's important to take care of yourself in order to maintain your energy and focus. Make time for activities that help you relax and recharge, such as exercise, meditation, or spending time with loved ones.

Finally, it's important to remember that conquering your limiting beliefs is a process, not a destination. It may take time and effort to overcome deeply ingrained beliefs, but by staying committed to your goals and focusing on growth and possibility, you can develop the resilience and perseverance necessary for achieving success.

To conquer your limiting beliefs, it's also important to cultivate a growth mindset. A growth mindset is the belief that your abilities can be developed through hard work, dedication, and perseverance. By embracing a growth mindset, you can view challenges as opportunities for growth and learning, rather than obstacles to be avoided.

One way to cultivate a growth mindset is to focus on the process of learning and development, rather than the end result. For example, if you have the limiting belief that "I'll never be able to master this skill," try to focus on the steps you can take to improve and learn, rather than the ultimate outcome. By focusing on the process of growth and development, you can reduce the impact of your limiting beliefs and build your confidence and resilience.

Another way to cultivate a growth mindset is to seek out feedback and constructive criticism. By seeking out feedback from others, you can gain valuable insights into your strengths and weaknesses, and identify areas where you can improve and grow. By embracing feedback as an opportunity for growth and learning, you can reduce the impact of your limiting beliefs and develop greater resilience and determination.

It's also important to celebrate your successes, no matter how small. By acknowledging your achievements and milestones, you can reinforce positive beliefs and build your confidence and motivation. Take time to reflect on your progress and celebrate your accomplishments, no matter how small they may seem.

Finally, it's important to remember that overcoming limiting beliefs is a process that requires patience, perseverance, and self-compassion. Be kind to yourself, and don't expect to overcome your limiting beliefs overnight. Remember that setbacks and challenges are a natural part of the journey, and that each one presents an opportunity for growth and learning.

In summary, conquering your limiting beliefs is an essential step in achieving success as a woman entrepreneur. By reframing your negative assumptions, taking action towards your goals, seeking out support and guidance, practicing self-care, cultivating a growth mindset, and celebrating your successes, you can overcome self-doubt and achieve greater success and fulfillment in your personal and professional life.

Breaking Free from the "Go to School, Get into College, Get a Good Job" Mindset

As a woman entrepreneur, you have the power to create your own path to success and fulfillment, beyond the traditional expectations of society.

As women, we're often taught to follow a certain path in life: go to school, get into college, and get a good job. While this may have been a successful path for some, it's not necessarily the only path to success. This mindset shift is very hard for some people to see, which is why you may receive pushback or discouragement from people you know. In fact, many successful women entrepreneurs have broken free from this traditional mindset and created their own paths to success.

Breaking free from the "go to school, get into college, get a good job" mindset involves challenging traditional assumptions about what it means to be successful. It requires a willingness to take risks, try new things, and step outside of your comfort zone. It places an emphasis on conformity and stability, rather than innovation and creativity. It involves breaking guidelines that your parents may have instilled in you which can be mentally tough.

One way to break free from this mindset is to explore your passions and interests. What excites you? What are you truly passionate about? By exploring your passions and interests, you can identify opportunities that align with your values and goals, and create a path to success that's uniquely your own.

Another way to break free from this mindset is to cultivate a growth mindset. A growth mindset is the belief that your abilities can be developed through hard work, dedication, and perseverance. By embracing a growth mindset, you can view challenges as opportunities for growth and learning, rather than obstacles to be avoided.

It's also important to develop an entrepreneurial mindset, which involves taking ownership of your life and your career. An entrepreneurial mindset means being proactive, taking risks, and seeking out opportunities for growth and development. It means being willing to fail and learn from your mistakes, and being open to new ideas and perspectives. An entrepreneurial mindset involved accepting control of your success in life and business. You are not stuck on a set salary, you are in complete control of the amount of income you want to have.

Breaking free from the "go to school, get into college, get a good job" mindset also requires a willingness to challenge traditional assumptions about gender roles and expectations. Women entrepreneurs often face unique challenges and barriers, but by challenging these assumptions and advocating for themselves and their businesses, they can create paths to success that are truly their own.

One way to challenge traditional assumptions is to seek out female role models and mentors who have already broken free from the traditional path to success. These individuals can offer valuable insights, guidance, and support as you navigate the challenges of entrepreneurship. These individuals have gone through a lot of the struggles, if not all of them, that you may experience, so having someone to help guide you through them will make your success an easier journey.

It's also important to be willing to take risks and try new things. This may involve stepping outside of your comfort zone and trying things that may not always succeed. But by taking risks and learning from your failures, you can build the resilience and perseverance necessary for achieving success as a woman entrepreneur. This best person to bet on is yourself because you are in control of the work that needs to be put in. So bet on yourself every time!

In summary, breaking free from the "go to school, get into college, get a good job" mindset is an essential step in achieving success as a woman entrepreneur. By exploring your passions and interests, cultivating a growth and entrepreneurial mindset, challenging traditional assumptions, seeking out role models and mentors, and being willing to take risks, you can create a path to success that's uniquely your own.

Overcoming Fear and Self-Doubt

Fear and self-doubt are common challenges that many women entrepreneurs face. Whether it's the fear of failure, the fear of not being good enough, or the fear of taking risks, these negative emotions can hold you back and prevent you from achieving your goals. However, with the right mindset and strategies, it's possible to overcome fear and self-doubt and achieve success as a woman entrepreneur.

One way to overcome fear and self-doubt is to practice self-compassion. Self-compassion means treating yourself with kindness and understanding, rather than criticism and judgment. By practicing self-compassion, you can reduce the impact of negative emotions and build your resilience and confidence.

Another way to overcome fear and self-doubt is to reframe negative thoughts and beliefs. For example, if you have the belief that "I'll never be good enough to succeed," try reframing it as "I may not be perfect, but

I'm capable of learning and growing." By reframing negative thoughts and beliefs, you can reduce their power over you and build a more positive mindset.

It's also important to take action towards your goals, even if you feel afraid or uncertain. Taking small steps towards your goals can help build your confidence and reduce the impact of fear and self-doubt. By breaking your goals down into manageable tasks and focusing on progress rather than perfection, you can build momentum and achieve success over time. I break all of my goals out into my weekly to-do list and I feel so accomplished as I get to cross the small actionable steps off the list to get closer to achieving my goal.

Another strategy for overcoming fear and self-doubt is to seek out support and guidance from mentors, peers, and advisors. These individuals can offer valuable insights, feedback, and support as you navigate the challenges of entrepreneurship. By surrounding yourself with positive, supportive people, you can build your confidence and resilience and overcome self-doubt and fear. Expressing your fear and asking how others may have overcome the same things will give you insight as your trying to navigate through.

It's also important to cultivate a growth mindset, which involves embracing challenges and setbacks as opportunities for growth and learning. By viewing challenges and failures as opportunities for growth, you can reduce the impact of fear and self-doubt and build greater resilience and determination.

Finally, it's important to practice self-care and prioritize your well-being. This may involve setting boundaries, practicing mindfulness, or engaging in activities that bring you joy and fulfillment. By taking care of yourself, you can reduce the impact of negative emotions and build the resilience and strength necessary for achieving success as a woman entrepreneur. I talk about self-care a lot because it is so important and often overlooked when talking about entrepreneurship. Entrepreneurship has it's challenges and you need to be in a emotionally healthy and also well rested to accomplish many of your goals. So don't forget to TAKE YOUR BREAK! After all, you earned it!

In summary, overcoming fear and self-doubt is an essential step in achieving success as a woman entrepreneur. By practicing self-compassion, reframing negative thoughts and beliefs, taking action towards your goals, seeking out support and guidance, cultivating a growth mindset, and practicing self-care, you can overcome self-doubt and fear and achieve greater success and fulfillment in your personal and professional life.

Conclusion

In this chapter, we've explored the concept of limiting beliefs and how to break through them. We've identified the limiting beliefs that are holding you back, learned how to reframe and conquer them, and discovered the freedom of living without self-imposed limitations. We've explored the importance of breaking free from the traditional "go to school, get into college, get a good job" mindset. We've discussed the limitations of this mindset, the benefits of pursuing entrepreneurship, and strategies for overcoming fear and self-doubt as you pursue your entrepreneurial dreams.

Now, it's time to take action. Take a moment to reflect on your own limiting beliefs. What stories are you telling yourself that are holding you back? How can you reframe those thoughts and replace them with positive affirmations?

Remember, gorgeous, you have the power to break through your limiting beliefs and achieve your biggest goals. Keep challenging yourself, taking action, and visualizing your success. Keep pushing past your fears and doubts, and stay focused and committed to your vision and goals. In the next chapter, we'll explore the power of networking and mentorship, and how surrounding yourself with the right people can elevate your entrepreneurial journey to new heights. Get ready to connect, collaborate, and soar!

"You gain strength, courage, and confidence by every
experience in which you really stop to look
fear in the face.
You must do the thing you think you cannot do."
— Eleanor Roosevelt

CHAPTER 4: THE POWER OF NETWORKING AND MENTORSHIP

Welcome to Chapter 4 of Think Big, Act Bold! In this chapter, we'll explore the power of networking and mentorship in your entrepreneurial journey. As the saying goes, "You are the average of the five people you spend the most time with." By surrounding yourself with the right people, you can elevate your mindset, skills, and success to new heights. You should be around people you can learn from and people who can learn from you.

In this chapter, we'll discuss the benefits of networking and mentorship, how to build a strong network, and how to find the right mentors to support your growth.

The Benefits of Networking and Mentorship

Networking and mentorship are two powerful tools for achieving success as a woman entrepreneur. By building a strong network of peers, mentors, and advisors, you can gain valuable insights, feedback, and support, and develop the skills and knowledge necessary for achieving your goals.

One of the key benefits of networking is the opportunity to connect with like-minded individuals and build relationships with others in your industry or field. By attending networking events, joining professional organizations, and participating in online communities, you can meet others who share your interests and goals, and build your network of contacts and potential collaborators.

Networking can also provide opportunities for learning and professional development. By attending conferences, workshops, and other events, you can gain valuable insights into emerging trends, best practices, and innovative strategies, and apply these insights to your own business.

Another important benefit of networking is the opportunity to build your brand and reputation. By cultivating relationships with others in your industry or field, you can increase your visibility and credibility, and establish yourself as a thought leader or expert in your area of expertise. As people learn more about what you have to offer they are able to spread your business to their networks.

Mentorship is another powerful tool for achieving success as a woman entrepreneur. By seeking out mentorship from experienced entrepreneurs or business leaders, you can gain valuable insights, feedback, and support, and develop the skills and knowledge necessary for achieving your goals. If you do not have a mentor you are making things harder for yourself. A good mentor can guide you through some of the hardest parts of entrepreneurships because chances are they have already been through them in their own journey.

Mentors can provide guidance and support in a variety of areas, from business strategy and marketing to leadership and personal development. They can offer advice, share their own experiences and insights, and serve as a sounding board for your ideas and challenges.

In addition to providing guidance and support, mentors can also offer valuable connections and opportunities. By introducing you to their own network of contacts, mentors can help you build your own network and gain access to new opportunities and resources.

Mentorship can also provide a sense of accountability and motivation. By setting goals and regularly checking in with your mentor, you can stay focused and accountable, and make progress towards your goals over time.

In summary, networking and mentorship are essential tools for achieving success as a woman entrepreneur. By building a strong network of peers, mentors, and advisors, and seeking out mentorship from experienced entrepreneurs or business leaders, you can gain valuable insights, feedback, and support, and develop the skills and knowledge necessary for achieving your goals.

Building a Strong Network

Building a strong network is essential for achieving success as a woman entrepreneur. By cultivating relationships with other professionals in your industry or field, you can gain valuable insights, feedback, and support, and develop the skills and knowledge necessary for achieving your goals.

One of the first steps in building a strong network is to identify your goals and the types of relationships you want to build. For example, you may want to connect with peers in your industry to exchange ideas and best practices, or you may want to connect with mentors or advisors to gain guidance and support.

Once you've identified your goals, it's important to be proactive in seeking out networking opportunities. This may involve attending conferences, workshops, and other events, joining professional organizations or industry groups, or participating in online communities or social media platforms.

When networking, it's important to be genuine and authentic in your interactions with others. Focus on building meaningful relationships based on shared interests and goals, rather than simply collecting business cards or connections.

It's also important to be strategic in your networking efforts. Focus on building relationships with individuals who can offer valuable insights, feedback, or support, and who share your values and goals. Be sure to follow up with contacts after events or meetings, and stay connected through regular communication and updates.

Another important aspect of building a strong network is to be willing to give back and offer support to others. By sharing your own knowledge and expertise, and offering support and guidance to others in your network, you can build stronger, more meaningful relationships over time.

It's also important to be open to new ideas and perspectives when networking. By engaging with individuals who have different backgrounds, experiences, and perspectives, you can broaden your own knowledge and understanding, and gain new insights and ideas for your own business.

Finally, it's important to prioritize relationship building and networking as an ongoing practice. Building a strong network takes time and effort, and requires ongoing investment and cultivation. By making networking a priority and investing in relationships over the long term, you can build a strong and supportive network that will help you achieve your goals and overcome challenges as a woman entrepreneur.

In summary, building a strong network is an essential component of achieving success as a woman entrepreneur. By being proactive, strategic, and genuine in your networking efforts, and by prioritizing relationship building over the long term, you can gain valuable insights, feedback, and support, and develop the skills and knowledge necessary for achieving your goals.

Finding the Right Mentors

Finding the right mentors is essential for achieving success as a woman entrepreneur. By seeking out guidance and support from experienced mentors, you can gain valuable insights, feedback, and advice, and develop the skills and knowledge necessary for achieving your goals.

One of the first steps in finding the right mentors is to identify your goals and the areas in which you need guidance and support. This may involve assessing your strengths and weaknesses, and identifying areas in which you want to develop your skills or knowledge.

Once you've identified your goals and areas of focus, it's important to seek out mentors who have experience and expertise in those areas. This may involve reaching out to individuals in your industry or field, attending events or conferences where you can connect with potential mentors, or joining mentorship programs or networking groups that can connect you with experienced professionals.

When seeking out mentors, it's important to be clear about what you're looking for and what you hope to gain from the relationship. Be prepared to share your goals and aspirations with potential mentors, and to be open and receptive to their feedback and guidance.

It's also important to find mentors who share your values and vision, and who are committed to supporting your growth and development over the long term. Look for mentors who are willing to invest time and energy in your development, and who are passionate about helping others achieve success.

Another important aspect of finding the right mentors is to be willing to learn and grow from their guidance and feedback. Be open to new ideas and perspectives, and be willing to challenge your own assumptions and beliefs in order to achieve your goals.

It's also important to maintain regular communication and follow-up with your mentors, and to be respectful of their time and expertise. Be sure to express your appreciation for their guidance and support, and to stay engaged and committed to your own growth and development over the long term.

Finally, it's important to remember that mentorship is a two-way street. As you develop your own skills and expertise, be sure to share your own insights and knowledge with others, and to be willing to give back to your own community and network.

In summary, finding the right mentors is an essential step in achieving success as a woman entrepreneur. By seeking out guidance and support from experienced mentors, and by being open and receptive to their feedback and guidance, you can gain valuable insights and develop the skills and knowledge necessary for achieving your goals.

Conclusion

In this chapter, we've explored the power of networking and mentorship in your entrepreneurial journey. We've discussed the benefits of building a strong network and finding the right mentors to support your growth.

Now, it's time to take action. Take a moment to reflect on your own networking and mentorship efforts. Are there areas where you could be more intentional or strategic? Are there potential mentors or collaborators that you've been hesitant to approach?

Remember, gorgeous, you have the power to elevate your entrepreneurial journey by surrounding yourself with the right people. Keep seeking out opportunities to connect, collaborate, and grow. In the next chapter, we'll dive into the importance of taking bold, decisive action and embracing the unknown. Get ready to step out of your comfort zone and into your greatness!

"Networking is not about just connecting people.
It's about connecting people with people,
people with ideas, and people with opportunities."
— Michele Jennae

CHAPTER 5: TAKING BOLD, DECISIVE ACTION

Welcome to Chapter 5 of Think Big, Act Bold! In this chapter, we'll explore the importance of taking bold, decisive action in your entrepreneurial journey. As an entrepreneur, you'll face many challenges and obstacles along the way. But the key to success is not avoiding these challenges, but rather embracing them and taking action in the face of uncertainty.

In this chapter, we'll discuss the benefits of taking bold action, how to overcome analysis paralysis, and the importance of embracing failure as a necessary step on the path to success.

The Benefits of Taking Bold Action

Taking bold action is essential for achieving success as a woman entrepreneur. By stepping outside your comfort zone and taking calculated risks, you can gain valuable insights, build your confidence, and achieve breakthrough results in your business and personal life. These bold actions sometimes come with a strong fear and a lot of what-ifs, so remember your positive speaking and your affirmations to get you through when you feel nervous.

One of the first benefits of taking bold action is the opportunity to gain new perspectives and insights. By stepping outside your comfort zone and trying new things, you can gain valuable feedback and learn from your successes and failures.

Taking bold action can also help you build your confidence and overcome fears and self-doubt. By proving to yourself that you are capable of achieving your goals and overcoming challenges, you can build your self-esteem and develop the resilience necessary for achieving long-term success.

Another important benefit of taking bold action is the opportunity to achieve breakthrough results. By setting ambitious goals and taking bold steps towards achieving them, you can push beyond your limitations and achieve results that you may have thought were impossible.

Taking bold action can also help you build your reputation and establish yourself as a thought leader or expert in your area of expertise. By pushing beyond the status quo and innovating in your industry or field, you can gain visibility and credibility, and position yourself as a leader and influencer.

Finally, taking bold action can also be personally fulfilling and rewarding. By pursuing your passions and taking bold steps towards achieving your goals, you can experience a sense of purpose and meaning in your work, and feel fulfilled by the impact you are making in the world.

Of course, taking bold action also involves risks and challenges, and it's important to approach bold action in a strategic and calculated manner. This may involve developing a plan and timeline for achieving your goals, seeking out guidance and support from mentors or advisors, and taking calculated risks that are aligned with your values and goals.

In summary, taking bold action is essential for achieving success as a woman entrepreneur. By stepping outside your comfort zone, pushing beyond your limitations, and taking calculated risks, you can gain valuable insights, build your confidence, and achieve breakthrough results in your business and personal life.

Overcoming Analysis Paralysis

Analysis paralysis is a common challenge for many women entrepreneurs. It can be easy to get caught up in analyzing every decision and weighing every possible outcome, to the point where it becomes difficult to take any action at all. However, overcoming analysis paralysis is essential for achieving success in your business and personal life.

One of the first steps in overcoming analysis paralysis is to identify the root causes of your indecision. This may involve assessing your fears and limiting beliefs, and identifying any factors that may be contributing to your analysis paralysis, such as perfectionism or a fear of failure.

Once you've identified the root causes of your indecision, it's important to develop strategies for overcoming these obstacles. This may involve challenging your limiting beliefs and developing a growth mindset, seeking out guidance and support from mentors or advisors, and taking small steps towards your goals in order to build momentum and gain confidence.

It's also important to develop a framework for decision-making that can help you prioritize your options and make more confident, strategic decisions. This may involve developing a set of criteria or metrics for evaluating your options, and using this framework to objectively assess the pros and cons of each option.

Another important aspect of overcoming analysis paralysis is to stay focused on your goals and priorities. By keeping your long-term vision and goals in mind, you can stay motivated and focused on taking action, even in the face of uncertainty or doubt.

It's also important to be willing to take calculated risks and learn from your failures. By accepting that failure is a natural part of the learning process, and by using your failures as opportunities to learn and grow, you can develop the resilience necessary for overcoming analysis paralysis and achieving your goals.

Finally, it's important to recognize that overcoming analysis paralysis is an ongoing practice. It may take time and effort to develop the skills and habits necessary for taking bold action and making confident decisions. However, by staying committed to your growth and development, and by being open to new ideas and perspectives, you can overcome analysis paralysis and achieve your goals as a woman entrepreneur.

In summary, overcoming analysis paralysis is essential for achieving success as a woman entrepreneur. By identifying the root causes of your indecision, developing strategies for overcoming these obstacles, and staying focused on your goals and priorities, you can build the skills and habits necessary for taking bold action and making confident decisions.

Embracing Failure

Embracing failure is a key component of achieving success as a woman entrepreneur. While it may be tempting to avoid failure at all costs, the truth is that failure is a natural part of the learning process, and is often a necessary step on the path to achieving your goals.

One of the first steps in embracing failure is to shift your mindset around failure. Rather than seeing failure as a negative outcome, it's important to view it as an opportunity for growth and learning. By embracing failure as a natural part of the learning process, you can develop the resilience and perseverance necessary for achieving your goals over the long term.

It's also important to recognize that failure is often the result of taking risks and pushing beyond your limitations. By embracing failure as a natural part of the risk-taking process, you can develop the courage and confidence necessary for taking bold action and achieving breakthrough results in your business and personal life.

Another important aspect of embracing failure is to use your failures as opportunities for learning and growth. This may involve reflecting on the factors that contributed to your failure, and using this information to adjust your strategy and approach moving forward. It may also involve seeking out feedback and guidance from mentors or advisors, and being open to new ideas and perspectives.

It's also important to remember that failure is not a reflection of your self-worth or potential. Rather than allowing failure to define you, it's important to stay focused on your goals and priorities, and to view failure as a temporary setback on the path to achieving your dreams.

Finally, it's important to be willing to take calculated risks and embrace uncertainty as a natural part of the entrepreneurial journey. By accepting that failure is a possibility, and by being willing to take risks and try new things, you can develop the skills and mindset necessary for achieving your goals and making a positive impact in the world.

In summary, embracing failure is essential for achieving success as a woman entrepreneur. By shifting your mindset around failure, using your failures as opportunities for learning and growth, and being willing to take calculated risks, you can develop the resilience, courage, and confidence necessary for achieving your goals and making a positive impact in the world.

Conclusion

In this chapter, we've explored the importance of taking bold, decisive action in your entrepreneurial journey. We've discussed the benefits of taking bold action, how to overcome analysis paralysis, and the importance of embracing failure as a necessary step on the path to success.

Now, it's time to take action. Take a moment to reflect on your own willingness to take bold action. Are there areas where you're holding back or avoiding risk? How can you push yourself to take bolder, more decisive action towards your goals?

Remember, gorgeous, taking bold action is the key to achieving your biggest dreams and living your best life. Keep pushing yourself out of your comfort zone, taking calculated risks, and embracing failure as a necessary step on the path to success. In the next chapter, we'll explore the power of resilience and perseverance, and how to bounce back from setbacks and challenges with grace and grit. Get ready to rise up, gorgeous, because the best is yet to come!

"You can't be that kid standing at the top of the waterslide, overthinking it. You have to go down the chute."
— Tina Fey

CHAPTER 6: THE POWER OF RESILIENCE AND PERSEVERANCE

Welcome to Chapter 6 of Think Big, Act Bold! In this chapter, we'll explore the power of resilience and perseverance in your entrepreneurial journey. As an entrepreneur, you'll face many setbacks and challenges, but the key to success is not avoiding these obstacles, but rather bouncing back from them with grace and grit.

In this chapter, we'll discuss the benefits of resilience and perseverance, how to cultivate these qualities in yourself, and the importance of self-care in the face of adversity.

The Benefits of Resilience and Perseverance

Resilience and perseverance are essential qualities for achieving success as a woman entrepreneur. By developing these qualities, you can overcome obstacles, bounce back from setbacks, and achieve your goals over the long term.

One of the key benefits of resilience and perseverance is the ability to overcome challenges and setbacks. As an entrepreneur, you will inevitably face obstacles and setbacks, such as market downturns, funding challenges, or unexpected competition. By developing resilience and perseverance, you can stay focused on your goals, maintain your motivation and drive, and find creative solutions to overcome these challenges.

Another important benefit of resilience and perseverance is the ability to adapt to change. As the business landscape evolves and new challenges arise, it's important to be able to pivot and adjust your approach as needed. By developing resilience and perseverance, you can adapt to change more easily, and maintain your focus and motivation even in the face of uncertainty.

Resilience and perseverance can also help you build your self-confidence and self-esteem. By persevering through challenges and setbacks, and achieving your goals despite obstacles, you can build a sense of self-efficacy and belief in your own abilities. This, in turn, can help you stay motivated and driven, and continue pushing towards your goals even in the face of adversity.

Another important benefit of resilience and perseverance is the ability to inspire and motivate others. By demonstrating resilience and perseverance in your own journey as an entrepreneur, you can serve as a role model and inspiration for others who are on a similar path. This can help build a community of support and encouragement, and help foster a culture of resilience and perseverance within your industry or field.

Finally, developing resilience and perseverance can be personally fulfilling and rewarding. By setting ambitious goals, persevering through challenges and setbacks, and achieving your dreams, you can experience a sense of purpose and meaning in your work, and feel fulfilled by the impact you are making in the world.

In summary, resilience and perseverance are essential qualities for achieving success as a woman entrepreneur. By developing these qualities, you can overcome obstacles, adapt to change, build your self-confidence, inspire others, and experience personal fulfillment and meaning in your work.

Cultivating Resilience and Perseverance

Cultivating resilience and perseverance is a process that involves developing the skills and habits necessary for overcoming obstacles and staying focused on your goals over the long term. Here are some strategies for cultivating resilience and perseverance as a woman entrepreneur:

1.	Develop a Growth Mindset: One of the first steps in cultivating resilience and perseverance is to develop a growth mindset. This means embracing challenges as opportunities for growth and learning, and seeing setbacks as temporary obstacles rather than permanent roadblocks. By adopting a growth mindset, you can develop the resilience and perseverance necessary for achieving your goals over the long term.

2.	Set Ambitious Goals: Setting ambitious goals can help motivate you to persevere through challenges and setbacks. When you have a clear vision of what you want to achieve, you can stay focused on your goals and maintain your motivation even in the face of adversity.

3.	Break Your Goals into Small Steps: Breaking your goals into small, manageable steps can make them feel more achievable and help you build momentum towards achieving them. By focusing on taking small steps each day, you can stay motivated and make progress towards your goals over time.

4.	Build a Supportive Network: Building a network of mentors, peers, and advisors can provide you with the guidance, support, and encouragement you need to persevere through challenges and setbacks. By surrounding yourself with people who believe in your potential, you can stay motivated and inspired to achieve your goals.

5.	Learn from Failure: Rather than allowing failure to defeat you, it's important to use it as an opportunity for learning and growth. By reflecting on your failures, identifying the factors that contributed to them, and using this information to adjust your approach moving forward, you can develop the resilience and perseverance necessary for achieving your goals over the long term.

6.	Practice Self-Care: Taking care of yourself physically, mentally, and emotionally can help you build the resilience and perseverance necessary for achieving your goals. This may involve getting enough sleep, eating a healthy diet, engaging in regular exercise, and taking time for relaxation and self-reflection.

7.	Stay Focused on Your Why: Finally, it's important to stay focused on your why - the purpose and meaning behind your work. By staying connected to your values and vision, you can stay motivated and inspired to persevere through challenges and setbacks, and achieve your goals over the long term.

In summary, cultivating resilience and perseverance is a key component of achieving success as a woman entrepreneur. By adopting a growth mindset, setting ambitious goals, building a supportive network, learning from failure, practicing self-care, and staying focused on your why, you can develop the resilience and perseverance necessary for achieving your dreams and making a positive impact in the world.

The Importance of Self-Care

Self-care is an essential component of maintaining your health and well-being as a woman entrepreneur. When you prioritize self-care, you can manage stress, improve your mental and physical health, and maintain the energy and focus you need to achieve your goals.

Here are some key reasons why self-care is so important for women entrepreneurs:

1. Stress Management: Running a business can be stressful, with long hours, high stakes, and a never-ending to-do list. By prioritizing self-care, you can manage stress and prevent burnout. This may involve practices such as meditation, exercise, or taking breaks throughout the day to recharge.

2. Improved Physical Health: When you neglect self-care, you may experience physical symptoms such as exhaustion, headaches, or chronic pain. By prioritizing self-care, you can improve your physical health and energy levels. This may involve practices such as eating a healthy diet, getting enough sleep, and engaging in regular exercise.

3. Mental Health: Running a business can also take a toll on your mental health, with high levels of stress, pressure, and uncertainty. By prioritizing self-care, you can improve your mental health and well-being. This may involve practices such as therapy, mindfulness, or taking time for hobbies and activities you enjoy.

4.   Increased Productivity: When you prioritize self-care, you can actually increase your productivity and focus. By taking breaks, engaging in physical activity, and managing stress, you can maintain the energy and focus you need to be productive and achieve your goals.

5.   Improved Relationships: Neglecting self-care can also impact your relationships with others. When you are stressed and exhausted, you may be more irritable or less patient with those around you. By prioritizing self-care, you can improve your relationships and maintain positive connections with those around you.

Here are some strategies for prioritizing self-care as a woman entrepreneur:

1.   Make Time for Self-Care: The first step in prioritizing self-care is to make it a priority. This may involve scheduling time for self-care activities such as exercise, meditation, or relaxation.

2.   Practice Mindfulness: Mindfulness can help you stay present and focused in the moment, reducing stress and promoting well-being. This may involve practices such as meditation, deep breathing, or mindful movement.

3.   Engage in Regular Exercise: Exercise can help you manage stress, improve physical health, and increase energy and focus This may involve activities such as walking, yoga, or strength training.

4.   Get Enough Sleep: Getting enough sleep is essential for maintaining physical and mental health. This may involve practices such as establishing a consistent bedtime routine, limiting screen time before bed, and creating a comfortable sleep environment.

5.   Connect with Others: Building positive connections with others can help promote well-being and reduce stress. This may involve spending time with loved ones, joining a community group, or networking with other entrepreneurs.

In summary, prioritizing self-care is essential for women entrepreneurs. By managing stress, improving physical and mental health, increasing productivity, and maintaining positive relationships, self-care can help you achieve your goals and make a positive impact in the world. By adopting self-care practices such as mindfulness, regular exercise, and getting enough sleep, you can prioritize your health and well-being, and cultivate the resilience and perseverance necessary for achieving your dreams.

Conclusion

In this chapter, we've explored the power of resilience and perseverance in your entrepreneurial journey. We've discussed the benefits of these qualities, how to cultivate them in yourself, and the importance of self-care in the face of adversity.

Now, it's time to take action. Take a moment to reflect on your own resilience and perseverance. Are there areas where you could be more resilient or persevere more effectively? How can you prioritize self-care in your entrepreneurial journey?

Remember, gorgeous, resilience and perseverance are the keys to bouncing back from setbacks and challenges with grace and grit. Keep cultivating these qualities in yourself, and don't be afraid to seek out support when you need it. In the next chapter, we'll explore the power of gratitude and how to cultivate a mindset of abundance and positivity. Get ready to give thanks, gorgeous, because the best is yet to come!

*"I can be changed by what happens to me.
But I refuse to be reduced by it."*
— Maya Angelou

CHAPTER 7: THE POWER OF GRATITUDE AND ABUNDANCE

Welcome to Chapter 7 of Think Big, Act Bold! In this chapter, we'll explore the power of gratitude and abundance in your entrepreneurial journey. As an entrepreneur, it's easy to get caught up in the hustle and bustle of daily tasks and goals. But taking the time to cultivate gratitude and abundance can transform your mindset and bring even greater success and joy to your life.

In this chapter, we'll discuss the benefits of gratitude and abundance, how to cultivate these qualities in yourself, and the importance of celebrating your wins along the way.

The Benefits of Gratitude and Abundance

Gratitude and abundance are powerful mindsets that can have a significant impact on your life and business as a woman entrepreneur. By cultivating an attitude of gratitude and abundance, you can shift your mindset from one of scarcity and lack to one of abundance and possibility. Here are some key benefits of cultivating gratitude and abundance:

1. Increased Happiness: Gratitude has been shown to increase happiness and well-being. When you focus on what you have and what you are grateful for, you can experience a greater sense of joy and contentment in your life and business.

2. Positive Thinking: When you cultivate a mindset of abundance, you focus on what is possible rather than what is lacking. This can help you maintain a positive outlook and approach challenges with a solution-oriented mindset.

3. Improved Relationships: When you approach your relationships with gratitude and abundance, you can build stronger connections with those around you. By appreciating and valuing others, you can create positive and supportive relationships that can benefit your business and personal life.

4. Increased Resilience: When you approach challenges with a mindset of abundance, you can develop greater resilience and perseverance. By focusing on what is possible and staying optimistic in the face of adversity, you can stay motivated and overcome obstacles.

5. Greater Creativity: When you approach your work with a mindset of abundance, you can tap into greater creativity and innovation. By seeing opportunities where others see challenges, you can develop new and innovative solutions to problems.

Here are some strategies for cultivating gratitude and abundance as a woman entrepreneur:

1. Start a Gratitude Practice: One of the best ways to cultivate gratitude is to start a daily gratitude practice. This may involve writing down three things you are grateful for each day, or simply taking a moment to reflect on the things in your life you appreciate and value.

2. Focus on Abundance: When you focus on abundance, you can shift your mindset from one of scarcity to one of possibility. This may involve reframing negative thoughts and focusing on what is possible rather than what is lacking.

3. Celebrate Your Wins: Celebrating your successes, no matter how small, can help you cultivate a sense of abundance and gratitude. By acknowledging your accomplishments, you can maintain a positive outlook and stay motivated.

4. Express Gratitude to Others: Expressing gratitude to others can help strengthen your relationships and build a sense of

community. This may involve sending a thank-you note or simply telling someone how much you appreciate them.

5. Stay Present: Cultivating gratitude and abundance requires staying present in the moment and focusing on the positive aspects of your life and business. This may involve mindfulness practices such as meditation, deep breathing, or simply taking a moment to pause and reflect on the good things in your life.

In summary, cultivating a mindset of gratitude and abundance can have significant benefits for women entrepreneurs. By increasing happiness, promoting positive thinking, improving relationships, increasing resilience, and boosting creativity, gratitude and abundance can help you achieve your goals and make a positive impact in the world. By adopting gratitude practices such as starting a daily gratitude journal, focusing on abundance, celebrating your successes, expressing gratitude to others, and staying present in the moment, you can cultivate a mindset of gratitude and abundance and achieve greater success and fulfillment in your life and business.

Cultivating Gratitude and Abundance

Cultivating gratitude and abundance is an ongoing practice that can have a significant impact on your life and business as a woman entrepreneur. Here are some ways to dive deeper into cultivating these mindsets:

1. Gratitude Journaling: One of the most effective ways to cultivate gratitude is to start a gratitude journal. Write down three things each day that you are grateful for, no matter how small or seemingly insignificant. This practice can help you focus on the positive aspects of your life and business and develop a sense of appreciation for all that you have.

2. Mindfulness Meditation: Mindfulness meditation is a powerful practice for cultivating gratitude and abundance. By focusing on the present moment and being aware of your thoughts and emotions, you can develop a greater sense of gratitude for the present moment and all that it offers.

3. Positive Affirmations: Positive affirmations can help you reframe negative thoughts and cultivate a sense of abundance. Repeat affirmations such as "I am abundant" or "I am grateful for all that I have" regularly to shift your mindset and focus on the positive aspects of your life and business.

4. Visualization: Visualization is a powerful tool for cultivating abundance. Visualize yourself living your dream life and running a successful business. See yourself achieving your goals and

enjoying the abundance that comes with success. This practice can help you stay motivated and focused on your vision.

5. Giving Back: Giving back to others can be a powerful way to cultivate gratitude and abundance. When you give back, you are acknowledging the abundance in your own life and sharing it with others. This can help you develop a sense of gratitude for all that you have and a greater sense of abundance.

6. Gratitude Walks: Taking a gratitude walk can be a simple yet powerful way to cultivate gratitude and abundance. Take a walk in nature and focus on the things you are grateful for, such as the beauty of the natural world or the support of loved ones. This practice can help you shift your mindset and develop a greater sense of appreciation for the present moment.

7. Gratitude Challenges: Participating in a gratitude challenge can be a fun and effective way to cultivate gratitude and abundance. Join a challenge that encourages you to focus on gratitude for a set period of time, such as 30 days. This can help you develop a consistent gratitude practice and see the benefits of cultivating this mindset.

In summary, cultivating gratitude and abundance is an ongoing practice that can have a profound impact on your life and business as a woman entrepreneur. By journaling, practicing mindfulness meditation, using positive affirmations, visualizing success, giving back, taking gratitude walks, and participating in gratitude challenges, you can develop a greater sense of appreciation for all that you have and a greater sense of possibility for all that is yet to come. Cultivating gratitude and abundance can help you stay motivated, focused, and resilient in the face of challenges, and can help you achieve your goals and make a positive impact in the world.

Celebrating Your Wins

As a woman entrepreneur, it's easy to get caught up in the day-to-day challenges of running a business and forget to celebrate your wins, no matter how small. Celebrating your successes is an important part of cultivating a mindset of abundance and gratitude, as well as staying motivated and positive in the face of challenges. Here are some tips for celebrating your wins:

1. Recognize and Acknowledge Your Accomplishments: Take a moment to acknowledge your accomplishments and the hard work that went into achieving them. Whether you landed a new client, launched a new product, or hit a revenue goal, it's important to take a moment to recognize the effort that went into your success.

2. Reflect on What You Learned: Reflecting on what you learned from your successes can help you grow and improve as an entrepreneur. What worked well? What didn't work as well? What can you do differently next time? By reflecting on your wins, you can learn from them and apply those lessons to future endeavors.

3. Share Your Successes with Others: Sharing your successes with others can help you stay motivated and build a supportive network of peers and mentors. Share your accomplishments on social media, in your newsletter, or with a friend or mentor. Celebrating your wins with others can help you feel validated and acknowledged for your hard work.

4. Treat Yourself: Celebrating your successes doesn't have to be a grand gesture, but treating yourself can be a powerful way to acknowledge your accomplishments. Treat yourself to a massage, a nice dinner, or something else that brings you joy and helps you recharge.

5. Set New Goals: Setting new goals can help you build momentum and keep your focus on the future. By celebrating your wins, you can use that momentum to set new goals and continue to grow and evolve as an entrepreneur.

In summary, celebrating your wins is an important part of cultivating a mindset of abundance and gratitude as a woman entrepreneur. By recognizing and acknowledging your accomplishments, reflecting on what you learned, sharing your successes with others, treating yourself, and setting new goals, you can stay motivated, positive, and focused on the future. Celebrating your wins can help you maintain a positive attitude in the face of challenges and stay motivated to achieve your goals and make a positive impact in the world.

Conclusion

In this chapter, we've explored the power of gratitude and abundance in your entrepreneurial journey. We've discussed the benefits of these qualities, how to cultivate them in yourself, and the importance of celebrating your wins along the way.

Now, it's time to take action. Take a moment to reflect on your own gratitude and abundance mindset. Are there areas where you could focus more on gratitude and abundance in your life? How can you celebrate your wins and cultivate a mindset of positivity and abundance?

Remember, gorgeous, gratitude and abundance are powerful tools for transforming your mindset and bringing greater success and joy to your life. Keep practicing gratitude, focusing on possibilities, and celebrating your wins along the way. In the next chapter, we'll explore the importance of staying true to your authentic self and embracing your unique gifts and talents. Get ready to shine, gorgeous, because the world needs your light!

*"Gratitude makes sense of our past,
brings peace for today,
and creates a vision for tomorrow."*
— Melody Beattie

CHAPTER 8: STAYING TRUE TO YOUR AUTHENTIC SELF

Welcome to Chapter 8 of Think Big, Act Bold! In this chapter, we'll explore the importance of staying true to your authentic self in your entrepreneurial journey. As an entrepreneur, it's easy to get caught up in the comparison game and try to emulate the successes of others. But the key to true success and fulfillment is staying true to your own unique gifts and talents. There is only one of you so embrace it and share it with the world!

In this chapter, we'll discuss the benefits of staying true to your authentic self, how to identify your unique gifts and talents, and the importance of creating a business that aligns with your values and purpose.

The Benefits of Staying True to Your Authentic Self

Staying true to your authentic self is crucial to your success and fulfillment as an entrepreneur. When you're true to yourself, you're able to tap into your own unique gifts and talents, which can bring even greater success and fulfillment to your life.

As a woman entrepreneur, it's important to stay true to your authentic self in order to build a successful and fulfilling business. Here are some of the benefits of staying true to your authentic self:

1. Increased Confidence: When you stay true to who you are, you can feel more confident in yourself and your abilities. This confidence can translate into all aspects of your life and business, from networking and marketing to making big decisions.

2. Greater Resilience: Staying true to your authentic self can help you weather the ups and downs of entrepreneurship with greater resilience. When you're aligned with your values and passions, you're better equipped to handle challenges and setbacks.

3. Stronger Relationships: Authenticity can help you build stronger and more meaningful relationships with clients, customers, and peers. People are drawn to authenticity and honesty, and being true to yourself can help you build trust and connection with others.

4. Increased Creativity: Staying true to your authentic self can help you tap into your unique perspective and creativity. By embracing your individuality, you can bring fresh ideas and perspectives to your business and stand out from the competition.

5. Improved Decision-Making: When you're in touch with your authentic self, you're better able to make decisions that are in alignment with your values and goals. This can lead to greater clarity and focus, and ultimately, better outcomes for your business.

6. Enhanced Well-Being: Being true to yourself can also have a positive impact on your overall well-being. When you're living and working in alignment with your authentic self, you're more likely to feel fulfilled, energized, and motivated.

In order to stay true to your authentic self, it's important to regularly check in with yourself and your values. Ask yourself what matters most to you and how you can align your business with those values. Surround yourself with supportive peers and mentors who share your values and encourage you to be your authentic self. Finally, don't be afraid to take risks and step outside of your comfort zone. Embrace your unique perspective and let it shine through in your business. By staying true to your authentic self, you can build a successful and fulfilling business that reflects who you truly are.

When you're true to yourself, you're also able to attract clients, customers, and partnerships that align with your values and purpose. This can create a more fulfilling and satisfying business experience, as you're able to work with people who share your vision and passion.

Identifying Your Unique Gifts and Talents

The first step in staying true to your authentic self is identifying your unique gifts and talents. Take some time to reflect on what comes naturally to you, what you enjoy doing, and what others have complimented you on in the past.

Identifying your unique gifts and talents is an important part of building a successful and fulfilling business. When you know what you're naturally good at, you can focus on those areas and create a business that plays to your strengths. Here are some tips for identifying your unique gifts and talents:

1. Look for Patterns: Think about the tasks and activities that come easily to you and that you enjoy doing. Look for patterns in these activities, and try to identify the skills and strengths that you're using. For example, if you enjoy writing, you might be naturally gifted in communication and storytelling.

2. Ask for Feedback: Sometimes it can be hard to identify our own strengths, so it's important to seek feedback from others. Ask friends, family, or colleagues what they think you're good at, or ask for feedback on a specific project or task.

3. Reflect on Your Past Experiences: Think about the experiences in your life that have been particularly fulfilling or successful. What strengths did you use in those experiences? How can you apply those strengths to your business?

4. Take Personality Tests: There are many personality tests available online that can help you identify your strengths and preferences. The Myers-Briggs Type Indicator and the StrengthsFinder assessment are two popular options.

5. Experiment: Finally, don't be afraid to experiment and try new things. Take on new projects or challenges, and pay attention to

what comes easily to you and what you enjoy. Over time, you'll start to develop a clearer picture of your unique gifts and talents.

Once you've identified your unique gifts and talents, it's important to find ways to leverage them in your business. This might mean delegating tasks that don't play to your strengths, or focusing your marketing efforts on the areas where you excel. By building a business that leverages your unique gifts and talents, you'll be more likely to experience success and fulfillment.

In summary, identifying your unique gifts and talents is an important part of building a successful and fulfilling business. By looking for patterns in your skills and strengths, seeking feedback from others, reflecting on past experiences, taking personality tests, and experimenting with new things, you can start to develop a clearer picture of what makes you unique. Once you've identified your strengths, it's important to find ways to leverage them in your business, whether that means delegating tasks, focusing your marketing efforts, or pursuing new opportunities that play to your strengths. By building a business that reflects your unique gifts and talents, you'll be more likely to experience success and fulfillment.

Creating a Business That Aligns with Your Values and Purpose

Creating a business that aligns with your values and purpose is a key component of building a successful and fulfilling venture. When you're clear on your values and purpose, you can create a business that reflects those priorities and helps you achieve your goals. Here are some tips for creating a business that aligns with your values and purpose:

1. Identify Your Core Values: Your core values are the principles and beliefs that guide your decisions and behaviors. Take some time to reflect on what's most important to you, and identify your top core values. These might include things like honesty, integrity, creativity, or community. Do you know what your core values are? If not, now is a great time to work on writing them out!

2. Clarify Your Purpose: Your purpose is the reason why you're in business - the impact you want to have on the world. Reflect on what drives you and what you're passionate about, and clarify your purpose. This might include a specific problem you want to

solve, a group of people you want to serve, or a particular vision for the future.

3. Build a Mission Statement: Your mission statement is a concise statement that describes what your business does, who it serves, and what makes it unique. Use your core values and purpose to guide the development of your mission statement, and make sure it aligns with your overall vision for your business.

4. Set Goals That Align with Your Values and Purpose: When you're setting goals for your business, make sure they align with your core values and purpose. This will help ensure that you're focused on the things that matter most to you, and that you're working towards a purpose that truly inspires you.

5. Make Decisions That Align with Your Values and Purpose: As you make decisions for your business, use your core values and purpose as a guide. Ask yourself whether each decision aligns with your values and purpose, and use that information to guide your choices.

By creating a business that aligns with your values and purpose, you'll be more likely to experience success and fulfillment. When your business is aligned with your priorities and passions, you'll be more motivated, more focused, and more effective. You'll also be more likely to attract customers and clients who share your values and appreciate what you have to offer.

In summary, creating a business that aligns with your values and purpose is essential for building a successful and fulfilling venture. By identifying your core values, clarifying your purpose, building a mission statement, setting goals that align with your values and purpose, and making decisions that reflect your priorities, you can create a business that reflects who you are and what you stand for. When your business is aligned with your values and purpose, you'll be more likely to achieve your goals, attract the right customers and clients, and experience success and fulfillment in your work.

Conclusion

In this chapter, we've explored the importance of staying true to your authentic self in your entrepreneurial journey. We've discussed the benefits of staying true to yourself, how to identify your unique gifts and talents, and the importance of creating a business that aligns with your values and purpose.

Now, it's time to take action. Take a moment to reflect on your own authentic self. Are there areas where you're trying to emulate the successes of others, rather than staying true to your own unique gifts and talents? How can you create a business that aligns with your values and purpose?

Remember, gorgeous, staying true to your authentic self is the key to true success and fulfillment as an entrepreneur. Keep identifying and cultivating your unique gifts and talents, and create a business that aligns with your values and purpose. In the next chapter, we'll explore the importance of setting boundaries and saying no to things that don't align with your vision and values. Get ready to stand in your power, gorgeous, because you've got this!

*"Gratitude makes sense of our past,
brings peace for today,
and creates a vision for tomorrow."
— Melody Beattie*

CHAPTER 9: SETTING BOUNDARIES AND SAYING NO

Welcome to Chapter 9 of Think Big, Act Bold! In this chapter, we'll explore the importance of setting boundaries and saying no in your entrepreneurial journey. As an entrepreneur, it's easy to get caught up in the endless demands of your business and neglect your own needs and priorities. But setting boundaries and saying no is crucial to maintaining your energy, focus, and motivation.

This chapter hits home for me! I struggled setting boundaries and saying no. I want to help everyone, and being a natural giver yes usually comes out before I even think. Once I became an full-time entrepreneur many people thought that meant "I didn't work", so they would ask me for favors or help thinking I'm not doing anything since I wasn't clocking into a job.

In this chapter, we'll discuss the benefits of setting boundaries and saying no, how to establish clear boundaries, and the importance of communicating your boundaries effectively.

The Benefits of Setting Boundaries and Saying No

If you are anything like me saying no is not an easy task. I'm a giver at heart and this was a huge mindset shift that I had to go through to find success in my business and my mental health.

Setting boundaries and saying no are essential practices for maintaining balance and well-being in both your personal and professional life. When you're able to set clear boundaries and say no to requests or opportunities that don't align with your priorities, you'll have more time and energy to focus on the things that matter most to you. Here are some benefits of setting boundaries and saying no:

1. Improved Time Management: By setting boundaries and saying no, you can prioritize your time and focus on the tasks and activities that are most important to you. This can help you become more productive and efficient, and ultimately achieve your goals more quickly.

2. Reduced Stress and Burnout: When you're able to say no to requests or opportunities that don't align with your priorities, you'll have more time and energy to devote to the things that matter most to you. This can help you avoid burnout and reduce stress, which can have a positive impact on your overall well-being.

3. Increased Confidence and Self-Esteem: Setting boundaries and saying no can also help you build confidence and self-esteem. When you're able to stand up for your own needs and priorities, you'll feel more empowered and in control of your life.

4. Better Relationships: By setting clear boundaries and communicating your needs and priorities to others, you can build stronger and healthier relationships. When you're able to say no to requests or opportunities that don't align with your priorities, you'll be more authentic and honest in your interactions with others, which can help build trust and respect.

Despite the many benefits of setting boundaries and saying no, it can be challenging to put these practices into action. Many people struggle with saying no, either because they don't want to disappoint others or because they fear missing out on opportunities. In my own experience, I've struggled with saying no in the past. I often found myself overcommitting and taking on too much, which left me feeling stressed and overwhelmed.

To overcome this challenge, I've had to learn to be more intentional about setting boundaries and saying no. This has involved getting clear on my priorities and values, and being willing to communicate those priorities and values to others. It's also involved learning to let go of the fear of missing out, and trusting that the opportunities that are meant for me will come my way.

One of the key challenges of setting boundaries and saying no is learning to overcome the fear of disappointing others. Many people struggle with this fear, which can stem from a variety of sources, such as a desire to be liked or a fear of conflict. However, it's important to remember that setting boundaries and saying no are not inherently negative actions. In fact, they can be a sign of self-respect and a way of honoring your own needs and priorities.

To overcome the fear of disappointing others, it can be helpful to reframe your mindset around setting boundaries and saying no. Instead of seeing them as negative actions, try to view them as positive steps towards taking care of yourself and living a life that aligns with your values. It can also be helpful to practice assertiveness skills, such as using "I" statements and setting clear expectations, to communicate your needs and priorities in a respectful and effective way.

Another key aspect of setting boundaries and saying no is learning to recognize when you're taking on too much. It's important to be honest with yourself about your capacity and to recognize when you need to take a step back or delegate tasks to others. This can involve setting realistic goals and deadlines, prioritizing tasks based on their importance and urgency, and learning to say no to requests or opportunities that don't align with your current priorities.

Finally, it's important to remember that setting boundaries and saying no are ongoing practices. As your priorities and circumstances change, you may need to adjust your boundaries and reevaluate your commitments. By staying flexible and adaptable, you'll be able to continue living a life that aligns with your values and priorities, even as your circumstances evolve.

In summary, setting boundaries and saying no are important practices for maintaining balance and well-being in both your personal and professional life. By improving your time management, reducing stress and burnout, increasing confidence and self-esteem, and building better relationships, you'll be able to live a more fulfilling and authentic life. While it can be challenging to put these practices into action, it's important to remember that they're essential for achieving your goals and living a life that aligns with your priorities and values. By learning to set clear boundaries and say no when necessary, you'll be able to create the time and space you need to focus on the things that matter most to you.

Establishing Clear Boundaries

Establishing clear boundaries is a key aspect of building healthy relationships, both in your personal and professional life. By setting and enforcing clear boundaries, you communicate your needs and expectations to others, which helps to establish mutual respect and trust. Here are some benefits of establishing clear boundaries:

1. Increased Self-Esteem: When you set and enforce clear boundaries, you communicate to others that your needs and priorities are important. This can help to build your self-esteem and self-worth, which can have a positive impact on all areas of your life.

2. Improved Relationships: Clear boundaries help to establish mutual respect and trust in relationships. When both parties understand and respect each other's boundaries, it creates a sense of safety and security, which can deepen the connection between them.

3. Better Communication: Establishing clear boundaries requires open and honest communication. By practicing clear and direct communication, you can avoid misunderstandings and build stronger, more meaningful relationships.

4. Reduced Stress: When you set clear boundaries, you can avoid situations that cause stress or conflict. By communicating your needs and priorities, you can create a sense of predictability and control in your life, which can reduce stress and anxiety.

Despite the many benefits of setting clear boundaries, it can be challenging to put these practices into action. Many people struggle with setting and enforcing boundaries, either because they fear conflict or because they don't want to disappoint others. However, setting and enforcing clear boundaries is essential for maintaining healthy relationships and a strong sense of self-worth.

To establish clear boundaries, it's important to start by identifying your needs and priorities. What are the things that are most important to you? What are the things that make you feel uncomfortable or stressed? Once you've identified your needs and priorities, you can communicate them clearly and directly to others. This might involve saying "no" to requests or opportunities that don't align with your priorities, or setting limits on your time or energy.

It's also important to practice assertiveness skills, such as using "I" statements and setting clear expectations, to communicate your needs and priorities in a respectful and effective way. This can involve expressing your thoughts and feelings clearly and honestly, while also being respectful of the needs and feelings of others.

Another key aspect of establishing clear boundaries is learning to enforce them consistently. This means setting consequences for boundary violations and following through on those consequences when necessary. By enforcing your boundaries consistently, you communicate to others that your needs and priorities are important and that you're willing to take action to protect them.

In summary, establishing clear boundaries is essential for building healthy relationships and maintaining a strong sense of self-worth. By identifying your needs and priorities, communicating them clearly and directly, and enforcing them consistently, you can create a sense of safety, security, and control in your life. While it can be challenging to put these practices into action, it's important to remember that they're essential for building healthy relationships and living a fulfilling life. Communicating Your Boundaries Effectively

Another important aspect of setting boundaries is communicating them effectively. Be clear and direct when communicating your boundaries, and avoid making excuses or apologizing for them. Remember, your boundaries are important and necessary to your success and well-being as an entrepreneur.

It's also important to be flexible and open to negotiation when necessary. While it's important to stick to your non-negotiables, there may be times when you need to adjust your boundaries to accommodate a new opportunity or partnership. The key is to be clear and direct in your communication, and to stay true to your priorities and values.

Conclusion

In this chapter, we've explored the importance of setting boundaries and saying no in your entrepreneurial journey. We've discussed the benefits of setting clear boundaries, how to establish your non-negotiables, and the importance of communicating your boundaries effectively.

Now, it's time to take action. Take a moment to reflect on your own boundaries and priorities. Are there areas where you're neglecting your own needs and priorities in favor of others' demands? How can you establish clearer boundaries around your time, energy, and priorities?

Remember, gorgeous, setting boundaries and saying no is crucial to maintaining your energy, focus, and motivation as an entrepreneur. Keep establishing clear boundaries, communicating them effectively, and prioritizing your own needs and goals. In the next chapter, we'll explore the importance of giving back and leaving a positive impact on the world through your business. Get ready to make a difference, gorgeous, because the world needs your light!

"Daring to set boundaries is about having
the courage to love ourselves,
even when we risk disappointing others."
— Brené Brown

CHAPTER 10: MAKING A POSITIVE IMPACT THROUGH YOUR BUSINESS

Welcome to chapter 10 of Think Big, Act Bold! In this chapter, we'll explore the importance of making a positive impact through your business. As an entrepreneur, you have the power to create change and make a difference in the world through your products, services, and values. My biggest goal is to make the world a better place than it was when I was born!

In this chapter, we'll discuss the benefits of making a positive impact, how to align your business with your values and purpose, and the importance of giving back to your community and the world.

The Benefits of Making a Positive Impact

Making a positive impact can have a powerful and lasting effect on both yourself and those around you. Whether it's through volunteering, mentoring, or creating a business that aligns with your values and purpose, there are many ways to make a positive impact in your community and the world. Here are some benefits of making a positive impact:

1. Increased Sense of Purpose: Making a positive impact can help to give your life a greater sense of purpose and meaning. When you contribute to something larger than yourself, it can help to give your life a sense of direction and focus.

2.   Improved Mental Health: Helping others can have a positive impact on your mental health. Studies have shown that volunteering, for example, can reduce symptoms of depression and anxiety and improve overall life satisfaction.

3.   Stronger Relationships: Making a positive impact can help to build stronger, more meaningful relationships. Whether it's through volunteering with others or creating a business that serves a community, working towards a shared goal can create a sense of connection and camaraderie.

4.   Increased Empathy and Compassion: Making a positive impact can help to cultivate empathy and compassion for others. By understanding and working to address the challenges faced by others, you can develop a deeper sense of empathy and a greater ability to connect with others.

5.   Improved Reputation: Making a positive impact can also help to improve your reputation, whether it's in your personal or professional life. By contributing to your community or creating a business that aligns with your values, you can build a reputation as someone who is committed to making a difference.

Despite the many benefits of making a positive impact, it can be challenging to put these practices into action. Many people struggle with finding the time or resources to make a meaningful contribution, or they may feel overwhelmed by the scale of the problems they want to address. However, making a positive impact doesn't have to be an all-or-nothing proposition. Even small acts of kindness or contributions can make a difference in someone's life.

To make a positive impact, it's important to start by identifying your values and passions. What are the things that matter most to you? What are the issues or causes that you care about most deeply? Once you've identified these values and passions, you can start to look for ways to contribute to them, whether it's through volunteering, donating to a cause, or creating a business that aligns with your values.

It's also important to remember that making a positive impact doesn't have to be a solo endeavor. By working with others who share your values and passions, you can amplify your impact and make a greater difference in your community and the world. This might involve joining a community group or organization, collaborating with others on a project, or seeking out mentorship or guidance from those who have experience in your chosen field.

In summary, making a positive impact can have a profound and lasting effect on both yourself and those around you. By identifying your values and passions, seeking out opportunities to contribute, and working with others who share your goals, you can create a sense of purpose and meaning in your life, improve your mental health and well-being, and make a lasting difference in your community and the world.
Aligning Your Business with Your Values and Purpose

The first step in making a positive impact through your business is aligning your business with your values and purpose. What is your why, or your reason for being an entrepreneur? What are the values that are most important to you and your business?

Once you've identified your values and purpose, it's important to integrate them into every aspect of your business, from your products and services to your marketing and communication. This can create a more authentic and purpose-driven brand, and enable you to attract customers and clients who share your vision and values.

Giving Back to Your Community and the World

Giving back to your community and the world can be one of the most rewarding experiences of your life. Whether it's through volunteering, donating to a cause, or creating a business that serves a greater purpose, there are many ways to give back and make a positive impact. Here are some benefits of giving back:

1. Increased Sense of Fulfillment: Giving back can give you a sense of purpose and fulfillment. When you contribute to a cause that is greater than yourself, it can help you feel like you are making a difference in the world.

2. Improved Mental Health: Giving back can also have a positive impact on your mental health. Studies have shown that volunteering can reduce symptoms of depression and anxiety and improve overall life satisfaction.

3. Building Stronger Connections: Giving back can help to build stronger connections with others. Whether it's through volunteering with a group of like-minded individuals or donating to a cause that you care about, giving back can create a sense of community and camaraderie.

4. Developing New Skills: Giving back can also help you develop new skills and experiences. Whether it's through volunteering or creating a business that serves a greater purpose, you can gain valuable experience and knowledge that can benefit you in your personal and professional life.

5. Making a Difference: Giving back can have a significant impact on your community and the world. By contributing your time, money, or resources, you can help to address important issues and make a lasting impact on those around you.

Despite the many benefits of giving back, it can be challenging to know where to start or how to make a meaningful contribution. Here are some tips for giving back:

1. Identify Your Passions and Values: Start by identifying the issues or causes that matter most to you. What are the things that you care about most deeply? What are the values that guide your life?

2. Research and Connect with Organizations: Once you've identified your passions and values, start researching organizations that align with those values. Look for volunteer opportunities or ways to donate to causes that are important to you.

3. Start Small: Giving back doesn't have to be a big or complicated endeavor. Start small by donating a small amount of money or volunteering for a few hours each month. Even small contributions can make a difference.

4. Collaborate with Others: Giving back can be more effective when done in collaboration with others. Consider joining a community group or organization, or working with others to create a business or project that serves a greater purpose.

5. Practice Gratitude: Finally, remember to practice gratitude for the opportunities you have to give back. Reflect on the impact

you are making and the positive changes you are helping to create in your community and the world.

In summary, giving back can have a profound and positive impact on your life and the world around you. By identifying your passions and values, connecting with organizations and communities, starting small, collaborating with others, and practicing gratitude, you can make a meaningful contribution to the causes that matter most to you and make a difference in the world.

Conclusion

In this chapter, we've explored the importance of making a positive impact through your business. We've discussed the benefits of aligning your business with your values and purpose, and the importance of giving back to your community and the world.

Now, it's time to take action. Take a moment to reflect on how you can make a positive impact through your business. How can you align your business with your values and purpose? How can you give back to your community and the world?

Remember, gorgeous, you have the power to create change and make a difference in the world through your business. Keep aligning your business with your values and purpose, and giving back to your community and the world. And above all, keep thinking big and acting bold, because the world needs your unique gifts and talents.

"You cannot get through a single day without
having an impact on the world around you.
What you do makes a difference,
and you have to decide what kind of
difference you want to make."
— Dr. Jane Goodall

CHAPTER 11: BUILDING A SUPPORTIVE NETWORK

Welcome to Chapter 11 of Think Big, Act Bold! In this chapter, we'll explore the importance of building a supportive network of mentors, peers, and advisors to help you navigate the challenges of entrepreneurship. As an entrepreneur, it's easy to feel isolated and overwhelmed, but building a supportive network can be the key to your success and well-being.

In this chapter, we'll discuss the benefits of a supportive network, how to identify and connect with mentors and advisors, and the importance of cultivating relationships with your peers.

The Benefits of a Supportive Network

Having a supportive network can be a critical factor in achieving success, both personally and professionally. Whether it's a group of peers, mentors, or advisors, a supportive network can provide you with the guidance, encouragement, and accountability needed to overcome challenges and reach your goals. Here are some benefits of having a supportive network:

1. Access to Knowledge and Expertise: A supportive network can provide you with access to a wealth of knowledge and expertise. Whether it's learning from the experiences of others, receiving advice from mentors, or connecting with experts in your field,

having a supportive network can help you develop the skills and knowledge needed to achieve your goals.

2.   Increased Confidence: Being a part of a supportive network can help increase your confidence and belief in yourself. When you surround yourself with people who believe in you and your abilities, it can help you overcome self-doubt and take bold action towards achieving your goals.

3.   Accountability and Motivation: A supportive network can also provide you with accountability and motivation. When you have people who are invested in your success and hold you accountable to your commitments, it can help you stay focused and motivated towards achieving your goals.

4.   Expanded Opportunities: Being a part of a supportive network can also expand your opportunities. Whether it's through introductions to new contacts or access to new resources, being a part of a supportive network can open up new possibilities and help you grow both personally and professionally.

5.   Emotional Support: Finally, a supportive network can provide you with emotional support during challenging times. When you have people who care about you and are there to listen and offer support, it can help you navigate through tough situations with greater ease.

Despite the many benefits of having a supportive network, it can be challenging to know where to start or how to build a strong network. Here are some tips for building a supportive network:

1.   Identify Your Needs: Start by identifying your needs and what you hope to gain from a supportive network. What skills or expertise do you need to develop? What challenges are you currently facing? Understanding your needs can help you identify the types of people you should seek out in your network.

2.   Attend Events and Join Groups: One of the best ways to build a supportive network is to attend events and join groups related to your interests and goals. Whether it's attending industry conferences, joining online communities, or participating in local meetups, these types of events can provide you with opportunities to meet new people and expand your network.

3.   Seek Out Mentors: Mentors can be a valuable source of guidance and support in your journey towards achieving your goals. Seek out mentors who have experience in your field and who can provide you with advice and feedback as you navigate through challenges and opportunities.

4.   Be a Good Listener: Being a good listener is an important trait for building strong relationships and networks. When you take the time to listen to others and understand their needs and goals, it can help you build stronger connections and foster a more supportive network.

5.   Give Back: Finally, giving back to your network can help strengthen your relationships and build a more supportive network. Whether it's offering your expertise or connections to help others achieve their goals, or simply providing emotional support during challenging times, giving back can help build a sense of reciprocity and support within your network.

In summary, having a supportive network can provide you with the guidance, encouragement, and accountability needed to achieve your goals and navigate through challenges. By identifying your needs, attending events and joining groups, seeking out mentors, being a good listener, and giving back, you can build a strong and supportive network that can help you succeed both personally and professionally.

Identifying and Connecting with Mentors and Advisors

Identifying and connecting with mentors and advisors can be a valuable resource for any entrepreneur. Whether you're just starting out or looking to take your business to the next level, mentors and advisors can provide you with guidance, support, and valuable insights that can help you navigate challenges and make strategic decisions. Here are some steps you can take to identify and connect with mentors and advisors:

1.   Define Your Goals: Before you start seeking out mentors and advisors, it's important to define your goals. What do you hope to achieve in your business? What areas do you need help with? By understanding your goals, you can identify the types of mentors and advisors who can best support you.

2.   Identify Potential Mentors and Advisors: Once you've defined your goals, it's time to identify potential mentors and advisors.

Look for people who have experience in your industry, who have achieved success in areas you want to improve in, and who have a track record of helping others achieve their goals.

3.   Reach Out: Once you've identified potential mentors and advisors, it's time to reach out to them. This can be done through networking events, social media, or email. Be clear about your goals and what you hope to achieve, and be respectful of their time.

4.   Build Relationships: Building strong relationships with your mentors and advisors is essential to getting the most out of the relationship. Take the time to get to know them, ask questions, and listen to their advice. Be open to feedback and be willing to implement their suggestions.

5.   Show Appreciation: Finally, it's important to show appreciation for your mentors and advisors. Thank them for their time and guidance, and let them know how much you value their support. This can help build a stronger relationship and encourage them to continue to support you in the future.

When identifying and connecting with mentors and advisors, it's important to remember that these relationships are two-way streets. While you can benefit greatly from their guidance and support, it's important to also be a valuable asset to them. By being proactive, respectful, and open to feedback, you can build strong and mutually beneficial relationships with your mentors and advisors.

Here are some benefits of having a strong network of mentors and advisors:

1.   Valuable Insights: Mentors and advisors can provide you with valuable insights into your industry, as well as strategies for achieving success.

2.   Access to Networks: Mentors and advisors often have their own networks of contacts that they can introduce you to, which can help you expand your own network.

3.   Accountability: Having a mentor or advisor can provide you with accountability to help you stay focused on your goals and make progress towards achieving them.

4. Emotional Support: Mentors and advisors can provide you with emotional support during challenging times, helping you stay motivated and focused on your goals.

5. Professional Development: Working with a mentor or advisor can help you develop new skills and knowledge, as well as learn from their experiences.

In conclusion, identifying and connecting with mentors and advisors can be a valuable resource for any entrepreneur looking to achieve success. By defining your goals, identifying potential mentors and advisors, reaching out, building relationships, and showing appreciation, you can build strong and mutually beneficial relationships that can help you navigate challenges and achieve your goals.

Cultivating Relationships with Your Peers

Cultivating relationships with your peers can be a valuable resource for any entrepreneur. While mentors and advisors can provide guidance and support, your peers can offer a different kind of support that can help you feel less isolated and provide a sounding board for ideas and challenges. Here are some ways you can cultivate relationships with your peers:

1. Attend Networking Events: Attending networking events can be a great way to meet other entrepreneurs and like-minded individuals. Look for events that are relevant to your industry or interests and be open to meeting new people.

2. Join a Mastermind Group: A mastermind group is a small group of individuals who meet regularly to discuss their challenges, goals, and strategies for success. Joining a mastermind group can help you build strong relationships with your peers and gain valuable insights and support.

3. Participate in Online Communities: There are many online communities for entrepreneurs, where you can connect with others who are facing similar challenges and share your experiences. Participating in online communities can be a great way to build relationships with your peers, even if you can't meet in person.

4.   Attend Conferences and Workshops: Attending conferences and workshops can be a great way to connect with other entrepreneurs and learn from experts in your field. Take advantage of networking opportunities and be open to meeting new people.

5.   Collaborate on Projects: Collaborating with other entrepreneurs on projects can be a great way to build relationships and expand your network. Look for opportunities to collaborate on projects that align with your interests and goals.

Here are some benefits of cultivating relationships with your peers:

1.   Support: Cultivating relationships with your peers can provide you with emotional support during challenging times, as well as feedback and advice on your ideas and challenges.

2.   Accountability: Having relationships with your peers can provide you with accountability to help you stay focused on your goals and make progress towards achieving them.

3.   Networking Opportunities: Building relationships with your peers can help you expand your network and connect with other individuals who can help you achieve your goals.

4.   Learning Opportunities: Your peers can offer valuable insights and knowledge that can help you learn and grow as an entrepreneur.

5.   Collaboration Opportunities: Building relationships with your peers can lead to collaboration opportunities that can help you achieve your goals and expand your business.

In conclusion, cultivating relationships with your peers can be a valuable resource for any entrepreneur. By attending networking events, joining mastermind groups, participating in online communities, attending conferences and workshops, and collaborating on projects, you can build strong relationships with your peers that can provide you with emotional support, accountability, networking opportunities, learning opportunities, and collaboration opportunities.

Conclusion

In this chapter, we've explored the importance of building a supportive network of mentors, peers, and advisors to help you navigate the challenges of entrepreneurship. We've discussed the benefits of a supportive network, how to identify and connect with mentors and advisors, and the importance of cultivating relationships with your peers.

Now, it's time to take action. Take a moment to reflect on your own network. Are there areas where you could benefit from the guidance and support of a mentor or advisor? How can you cultivate relationships with your peers and build a supportive community around your business?

Remember, gorgeous, building a supportive network is crucial to your success and well-being as an entrepreneur. Keep seeking out guidance and support from mentors and advisors, and cultivate relationships with your peers. In the next chapter, we'll explore the importance of embracing failure and taking bold action to achieve your goals and dreams. Get ready to step outside your comfort zone, gorgeous, because the world needs your unique gifts and talents!

"Surround yourself with only people
who are going to lift you higher."
— Oprah Winfrey

CHAPTER 12: OVERCOMING FEAR, SELF-DOUBT, AND IMPOSTER SYNDROME

Welcome to Chapter 12 of Think Big, Act Bold! In this chapter, we'll explore strategies for managing and overcoming fear, self-doubt, and imposter syndrome, which are common challenges for many women entrepreneurs. As an entrepreneur, it's normal to experience fear and self-doubt, but it's important not to let these emotions hold you back from achieving your goals and dreams.

In this chapter, we'll discuss the common causes of fear, self-doubt, and imposter syndrome, how to manage these emotions, and strategies for building confidence and self-belief.

The Causes of Fear, Self-Doubt, and Imposter Syndrome

As an entrepreneur, it is common to experience fear, self-doubt, and imposter syndrome. These feelings can be crippling and prevent you from achieving your goals. Understanding the causes of these feelings can help you overcome them and achieve success in your business.

1. Comparison: One of the biggest causes of fear, self-doubt, and imposter syndrome is comparison. When you compare yourself to others, you often feel inadequate and start to doubt your abilities. It is important to remember that everyone has their own journey and comparing yourself to others is not productive.

2. Perfectionism: Another cause of fear, self-doubt, and imposter syndrome is perfectionism. When you strive for perfection, you set unrealistic expectations for yourself, which can lead to feelings of inadequacy and self-doubt.

3. Past Experiences: Past experiences can also contribute to fear, self-doubt, and imposter syndrome. If you have experienced failure or rejection in the past, you may be more likely to doubt your abilities and fear failure in the future.

4. Lack of Support: A lack of support can also contribute to feelings of self-doubt and imposter syndrome. If you do not have a strong support system, you may feel like you are on your own and doubt your ability to succeed.

5. Negative Self-Talk: Negative self-talk can also contribute to fear, self-doubt, and imposter syndrome. When you constantly tell yourself that you are not good enough or that you will fail, you start to believe it and feel like an imposter.

It is important to identify the causes of your fear, self-doubt, and imposter syndrome so that you can address them and overcome them. Here are some strategies for overcoming these feelings:

1. Practice Self-Compassion: Practicing self-compassion is an important part of overcoming fear, self-doubt, and imposter syndrome. Instead of being hard on yourself, be kind and understanding.

2. Reframe Your Thoughts: Reframing your thoughts is another strategy for overcoming these feelings. Instead of focusing on your shortcomings, focus on your strengths and accomplishments.

3. Take Action: Taking action is an important step in overcoming fear, self-doubt, and imposter syndrome. When you take action, you gain confidence and momentum towards your goals.

4. Seek Support: Seeking support is also important in overcoming these feelings. Surround yourself with people who believe in you and can provide encouragement and support.

5.   Practice Gratitude: Practicing gratitude is another strategy for overcoming fear, self-doubt, and imposter syndrome. When you focus on the things you are grateful for, you are less likely to focus on your shortcomings.

In conclusion, fear, self-doubt, and imposter syndrome are common challenges for many women entrepreneurs. Understanding the causes of these feelings and implementing strategies to overcome them can help you achieve success in your business. By practicing self-compassion, reframing your thoughts, taking action, seeking support, and practicing gratitude, you can overcome these feelings and achieve your goals.

Managing Fear, Self-Doubt, and Imposter Syndrome

As an entrepreneur, managing fear, self-doubt, and imposter syndrome can be a daily challenge. These feelings can arise at any time, especially when faced with new challenges or stepping outside of your comfort zone. However, there are strategies that can help you manage these feelings and prevent them from hindering your progress.

1.   Recognize the Signs: The first step in managing fear, self-doubt, and imposter syndrome is to recognize the signs. You may feel anxious, have negative self-talk, or avoid taking risks. Recognizing these signs can help you take action to manage these feelings.
2.   Reframe Your Thoughts: Reframing your thoughts is an effective strategy for managing these feelings. When you have negative self-talk, try to reframe your thoughts by focusing on your strengths and accomplishments. Remember, everyone experiences setbacks and failures, and it is important to learn from these experiences and move forward.
3.   Take Action: Taking action is another effective strategy for managing these feelings. When you take action, you gain confidence and momentum towards your goals. Break down your goals into smaller, manageable tasks and take action towards them every day.
4.   Practice Self-Care: Practicing self-care is important for managing these feelings. Take time for yourself to relax and recharge, whether that means practicing yoga, meditating, or taking a walk outside. By taking care of yourself, you can better manage stress and anxiety.
5.   Seek Support: Seeking support is also important in managing these feelings. Surround yourself with people who believe in you

and can provide encouragement and support. Consider joining a networking group or finding a mentor who can provide guidance and support.

6. Embrace Failure: Embracing failure is another strategy for managing these feelings. Instead of fearing failure, embrace it as an opportunity to learn and grow. Failure is a natural part of the entrepreneurial journey, and by learning from your mistakes, you can become a better entrepreneur.

7. Break Down Your Goals: Another helpful strategy is to break down your goals into smaller, achievable steps. This can help you build momentum and confidence, and make it easier to tackle bigger challenges.

8. Celebrate Your Wins: Finally, it is important to celebrate your wins, no matter how small. Celebrating your accomplishments can help boost your confidence and provide motivation to keep moving forward.

In conclusion, managing fear, self-doubt, and imposter syndrome is an ongoing challenge for many women entrepreneurs. By recognizing the signs, reframing your thoughts, taking action, practicing self-care, seeking support, embracing failure, and celebrating your wins, you can effectively manage these feelings and achieve success in your business. Remember, everyone experiences these feelings at some point, but by implementing these strategies, you can overcome them and achieve your goals.

Building Confidence and Self-Belief

Building confidence and self-belief are essential for success as an entrepreneur. When you have confidence in yourself and your abilities, you are more likely to take risks, embrace challenges, and pursue your goals with determination.

Here are some strategies for building confidence and self-belief:

1. Identify Your Strengths: Recognizing your strengths is the first step in building confidence and self-belief. Take some time to reflect on your skills, accomplishments, and what makes you

unique. Write down a list of your strengths and remind yourself of them regularly.

2.   Set Goals: Setting goals is another effective strategy for building confidence and self-belief. When you set achievable goals and work towards them, you gain a sense of accomplishment and confidence in your abilities. Break down your goals into smaller, manageable tasks and celebrate your progress along the way.

3.   Embrace Challenges: Embracing challenges is an important part of building confidence and self-belief. When you step outside of your comfort zone and take on new challenges, you prove to yourself that you are capable of achieving great things.

4.   Learn from Failure: Failure is a natural part of the entrepreneurial journey, but it can also be an opportunity for growth and learning. When you experience failure, take the time to reflect on what went wrong and what you can do differently next time. Use your failures as an opportunity to learn and grow, rather than as a setback.

5.   Practice Self-Care: Practicing self-care is also important for building confidence and self-belief. Take time for yourself to relax and recharge, whether that means practicing yoga, meditating, or taking a walk outside. By taking care of yourself, you can better manage stress and anxiety, which can affect your confidence and self-belief.

6.   Surround Yourself with Positive People: Surrounding yourself with positive, supportive people is also important for building confidence and self-belief. Seek out mentors, advisors, and peers who believe in you and can provide encouragement and support along the way.

7.   Take Action: Finally, taking action is essential for building confidence and self-belief. When you take action towards your goals, even small steps, you gain momentum and confidence in your abilities. Don't be afraid to take risks and try new things - each action you take is a step towards building your confidence and self-belief.

In conclusion, building confidence and self-belief is essential for success as an entrepreneur. By identifying your strengths, setting goals, embracing challenges, learning from failure, practicing self-care, surrounding yourself with positive people, and taking action, you can build the confidence and self-belief necessary to achieve your goals and succeed in your business. Remember, building confidence and self-belief is an ongoing process, but with practice and dedication, you can become a more confident and successful entrepreneur.

Conclusion

In this chapter, we've explored strategies for managing and overcoming fear, self-doubt, and imposter syndrome, which are common challenges for many women entrepreneurs. We've discussed the causes of these emotions, how to manage them, and strategies for building confidence and self-belief.

Now, it's time to take action. Take a moment to reflect on your own experiences with fear, self-doubt, and imposter syndrome. Are there areas where you're holding yourself back due to these emotions? How can you challenge these negative thought patterns and build confidence and self-belief?

Remember, gorgeous, fear and self-doubt are natural emotions, but they don't have to hold you back from achieving your goals and dreams. Keep practicing positive self-talk and reframing your thoughts, and surround yourself with positive, supportive people. In the next chapter, we'll explore the importance of taking bold action and embracing failure as a necessary part of the entrepreneurial journey. Get ready to step outside your comfort zone, gorgeous, because you're capable of achieving greatness!

"It's not the absence of fear, it's overcoming it.
Sometimes you've got to blast through
and have faith."
— Emma Watson

CHAPTER 13: MARKETING AND BRANDING YOUR BUSINESS

Welcome to Chapter 13 of Think Big, Act Bold! In this chapter, we'll explore tips and best practices for marketing and branding your business. As a woman entrepreneur, building a strong and recognizable brand is essential for attracting your ideal clients and customers.

In this chapter, we'll discuss how to create a compelling brand story, the importance of social media in marketing, strategies for content marketing, and other best practices for effective marketing and branding.

Creating a Compelling Brand Story

Creating a compelling brand story is essential for any business. Your brand story is the narrative that defines who you are, what you stand for, and why you do what you do. A powerful brand story can differentiate you from your competitors, attract customers, and build a loyal following. Here are some strategies for creating a compelling brand story:

1. Define Your Mission and Values: Your brand story should be rooted in your mission and values. Take the time to define what you stand for, what you hope to achieve, and how you want to make a difference in the world. Your mission and values will form the foundation of your brand story.

2. Identify Your Target Audience: Knowing your target audience is key to creating a compelling brand story. Consider who your ideal customer is, what they care about, and what challenges they face. Your brand story should resonate with your target audience and speak directly to their needs and desires.

3. Craft Your Narrative: Once you have a clear understanding of your mission, values, and target audience, it's time to craft your narrative. Your brand story should be a clear, concise, and engaging narrative that captures the essence of your business. Use storytelling techniques to create a memorable and emotional connection with your audience.

4. Be Authentic: Authenticity is essential when it comes to creating a compelling brand story. Be honest and transparent about who you are, what you stand for, and what you hope to achieve. Don't try to be something you're not or make promises you can't keep. Your audience will appreciate your authenticity and be more likely to trust and engage with your brand.

5. Use Visuals: Visuals can be a powerful way to convey your brand story. Use images, videos, and other visual elements to bring your narrative to life. Choose visuals that align with your brand's values and resonate with your audience.

6. Be Consistent: Consistency is key when it comes to building a strong brand story. Ensure that your brand story is reflected in all aspects of your business, from your website and social media presence to your products and customer service. Consistency will help reinforce your brand's values and message, and build a strong and loyal following.

7. Evolve Your Story: Your brand story is not set in stone - it will evolve over time as your business grows and changes. Be open to revisiting and refining your narrative as needed. As your business evolves, your brand story should evolve with it to remain relevant and engaging.

In conclusion, creating a compelling brand story is essential for any business. By defining your mission and values, identifying your target audience, crafting a narrative, being authentic, using visuals, being consistent, and evolving your story, you can create a brand story that resonates with your audience, builds loyalty, and drives success.

Remember, your brand story is an ongoing process - continue to refine and evolve it as your business grows and changes.

The Importance of Social Media in Marketing

Social media is a powerful tool for marketing and branding your business. It allows you to connect with your target audience, share your brand story, promote your products and services, and engage with customers. Here are some key reasons why social media is important in marketing:

1. Increased Visibility: Social media allows businesses to reach a larger audience than traditional marketing methods. With over 3.8 billion active social media users worldwide, it provides a platform for businesses to showcase their products and services to a global audience.

2. Targeted Advertising: Social media platforms allow businesses to target their advertising to specific audiences based on demographics, interests, and behavior. This ensures that the right message is reaching the right people, resulting in more effective and efficient advertising.

3. Brand Building: Social media provides businesses with the opportunity to build and promote their brand in a way that is authentic and engaging. By creating content that resonates with their audience and aligns with their brand values, businesses can create a strong and recognizable brand identity.

4. Customer Engagement: Social media allows businesses to interact with their customers in real-time, providing a platform for feedback, support, and engagement. This creates a sense of community around the brand and can lead to increased loyalty and advocacy.

5. Cost-Effective: Social media marketing is often more cost-effective than traditional marketing methods, making it accessible to businesses of all sizes. Many social media platforms offer free business profiles, with advertising options available at a range of price points.

6. Analytics and Insights: Social media platforms provide businesses with a wealth of data and insights that can be used to

optimize their marketing strategy. This includes information on audience demographics, engagement rates, and content performance.

7. Mobile-Friendly: Social media is inherently mobile-friendly, making it an ideal platform for businesses looking to reach customers on-the-go. With more than 3.6 billion people using smartphones worldwide, social media provides businesses with the ability to reach customers wherever they are.

In conclusion, social media is a powerful tool for businesses looking to build their brand, engage with customers, and drive sales. By leveraging the benefits of increased visibility, targeted advertising, brand building, customer engagement, cost-effectiveness, analytics, and mobile-friendliness, businesses can create a successful social media marketing strategy. Remember, social media is an ongoing process - continue to refine and evolve your strategy to stay ahead of the curve and achieve success.

Strategies for Content Marketing

Content marketing is a key component of any successful social media marketing strategy. It involves creating and sharing valuable, relevant, and consistent content to attract and retain a clearly defined audience - ultimately driving profitable customer action. Here are some strategies for effective content marketing:

1. Know Your Audience: The first step in creating effective content is to understand your audience. Who are they? What are their interests, pain points, and challenges? What kind of content do they prefer? By answering these questions, you can tailor your content to resonate with your target audience.

2. Create a Content Calendar: Planning ahead is key to consistent and effective content creation. Create a content calendar to map out your content strategy for the upcoming weeks or months. This will ensure that your content is timely, relevant, and aligned with your overall marketing objectives.

3. Mix Up Your Content Formats: There are many different types of content that you can create, including blog posts, videos, infographics, podcasts, and more. Mixing up your content formats can help keep your audience engaged and interested.

4. Optimize for SEO: Search engine optimization (SEO) is the practice of optimizing your content to improve its ranking on search engine results pages. This can help drive more traffic to your website and increase visibility for your brand. Some key SEO tactics for content marketing include incorporating relevant keywords, optimizing title tags and meta descriptions, and building high-quality backlinks.

5. Promote Your Content: Creating great content is only half the battle - you also need to promote it to reach your audience. Share your content on social media, email newsletters, and other relevant channels. You can also consider paid promotion options, such as social media advertising or Google Ads.

6. Engage with Your Audience: Content marketing is a two-way street - it's not just about pushing content out, but also engaging with your audience. Respond to comments and messages, ask for feedback, and encourage user-generated content.

7. Measure Your Results: Finally, it's important to measure the success of your content marketing efforts. Use analytics tools to track metrics such as website traffic, engagement rates, and conversion rates. This will help you identify what's working and what's not, so you can refine your strategy for even better results.

By implementing these strategies, you can create a successful content marketing strategy that helps build your brand, engage with your audience, and drive profitable customer action. Remember, content marketing is an ongoing process - continue to refine and evolve your strategy to stay ahead of the curve and achieve success.

Other Best Practices for Effective Marketing and Branding

In addition to social media and content marketing, there are other best practices for effective marketing and branding. These include:

- Networking: Building relationships with other professionals and entrepreneurs can help you expand your reach and connect with potential clients and customers.
- Branding consistency: Consistency is key when it comes to branding. Make sure your branding is consistent across all

platforms and channels, from your website and social media profiles to your business cards and promotional materials.

- Customer service: Providing excellent customer service is essential for building a strong brand and reputation. Make sure you respond promptly to inquiries and concerns, and go above and beyond to meet your customers' needs and expectations.
- Analytics and metrics: Use analytics and metrics to track the effectiveness of your marketing and branding efforts. This may include tracking website traffic, social media engagement, or sales conversions.

Here are some strategies to consider when trying to incorporate these best practices:

1. Define Your Brand: Before you can effectively market and brand your business, you need to have a clear understanding of your brand identity. This includes your brand values, personality, voice, and visual identity. Once you have a clear understanding of your brand, you can ensure that all of your marketing efforts are consistent with your brand identity.

2. Create a Compelling Website: Your website is often the first point of contact between your business and potential customers, so it's essential to make a great first impression. Ensure that your website is visually appealing, easy to navigate, and optimized for search engines. It should also clearly communicate your brand value proposition and offer a seamless user experience.

3. Leverage Social Media: Social media platforms provide a powerful opportunity to connect with your audience and promote your brand. Identify which platforms your target audience is most active on, and create a content strategy that is tailored to each platform. Use social media to engage with your audience, share valuable content, and build brand awareness.

4. Utilize Influencer Marketing: Influencer marketing involves partnering with individuals who have a large and engaged following on social media, in order to promote your brand or product. This can be an effective way to reach new audiences and build credibility for your brand. When selecting influencers, ensure that they align with your brand values and have a genuine connection with their audience.

5.   Invest in Email Marketing: Email marketing remains one of the most effective ways to engage with your audience and drive conversions. Use email to nurture leads, promote your products or services, and communicate with your audience. Personalization and segmentation can help ensure that your emails are relevant and valuable to each recipient.

6.   Attend Events and Conferences: Attending events and conferences can provide valuable opportunities to network with peers, connect with potential customers, and promote your brand. Look for events that are relevant to your industry or target audience, and prepare to make a strong impression.

7.   Monitor and Measure Your Results: It's essential to monitor and measure the effectiveness of your marketing and branding efforts. Use analytics tools to track metrics such as website traffic, social media engagement, and email open rates. This will help you identify what's working and what's not, so you can refine your strategy for even better results.

By implementing these best practices, you can create an effective marketing and branding strategy that helps build your brand, engage with your audience, and drive profitable customer action. Remember, marketing and branding are ongoing processes - continue to refine and evolve your strategy to stay ahead of the curve and achieve success.

Conclusion

In this chapter, we've explored tips and best practices for marketing and branding your business. We've discussed how to create a compelling brand story, the importance of social media in marketing, strategies for content marketing, and other best practices for effective marketing and branding.

Remember, gorgeous, building a strong and recognizable brand is essential for attracting your ideal clients and customers. Keep refining and revisiting your brand story and marketing strategies, and don't be afraid to experiment and try new things.

In addition to the strategies we've discussed in this chapter, there are many other marketing and branding tactics you can explore. These may include email marketing, search engine optimization (SEO), paid advertising, or public relations.

It's important to stay up-to-date on the latest trends and best practices in marketing and branding, and to continually refine and adapt your strategies as your business evolves.

"Your brand is the single most important investment you can make in your business."
— Steve Forbes

CHAPTER 14: SELF-CARE AND WELLNESS PRACTICES FOR ENTREPRENEURS

Welcome to Chapter 14 of Think Big, Act Bold! In this chapter, we'll explore the importance of self-care and wellness practices for maintaining your energy, focus, and resilience as an entrepreneur. As an entrepreneur, it's easy to get caught up in the hustle and grind, but neglecting your well-being can lead to burnout and decreased productivity.

In this chapter, we'll discuss the benefits of self-care and wellness practices, and provide tips for incorporating self-care into your daily routine.

The Benefits of Self-Care and Wellness Practices

As a busy entrepreneur, it can be easy to neglect self-care and wellness practices in favor of focusing solely on your business. However, taking care of your physical, emotional, and mental health is essential to your overall well-being and success as an entrepreneur. Here are some of the key benefits of prioritizing self-care and wellness practices:

1. Increased Energy and Productivity: When you take care of your body and mind, you're better equipped to tackle the challenges of entrepreneurship. Engaging in regular exercise, getting enough

sleep, and eating a healthy diet can help boost your energy levels and increase your productivity.

2. Reduced Stress and Anxiety: Running a business can be stressful, and stress can take a toll on your physical and mental health. Prioritizing self-care and wellness practices such as meditation, yoga, or massage can help reduce stress and anxiety levels, allowing you to approach your work with a clearer and more focused mind.

3. Improved Creativity and Innovation: Taking a break from work and engaging in activities that inspire and energize you can help boost creativity and innovation. This can lead to new ideas and approaches for your business, helping you stay ahead of the competition.

4. Better Decision-Making: When you're exhausted or stressed, it can be challenging to make sound decisions for your business. Prioritizing self-care and wellness practices can help clear your mind and improve your ability to make informed and rational decisions.

5. Stronger Relationships: Taking care of your emotional and mental health can also benefit your personal relationships. When you're happy and fulfilled outside of work, you're more likely to build and maintain strong connections with loved ones, friends, and colleagues.

6. Increased Resilience: Running a business comes with its share of ups and downs. Prioritizing self-care and wellness practices can help increase your resilience and ability to bounce back from setbacks, which is critical for success as an entrepreneur.

Some self-care and wellness practices to consider include:

1. Regular exercise or movement, such as going for a walk or practicing yoga

2. Mindfulness practices such as meditation or journaling

3. Spending time outdoors and connecting with nature

4. Eating a balanced and healthy diet

5. Getting enough sleep and establishing a consistent sleep routine

6. Taking regular breaks and time off to recharge

7. Seeking support from a therapist or counselor, if needed

It's essential to remember that self-care and wellness practices are not selfish or indulgent - they're necessary for your overall well-being and success. By prioritizing self-care, you can improve your physical, emotional, and mental health, and be better equipped to tackle the challenges of entrepreneurship.

Incorporating Self-Care into Your Daily Routine

Incorporating self-care practices into your daily routine can seem daunting, especially when you have a business to run. However, small, intentional changes to your daily routine can make a big difference in your overall well-being. Here are some tips for incorporating self-care into your daily routine:

1. Make it a Priority: First and foremost, make self-care a priority. Schedule time for self-care activities just as you would schedule time for work-related tasks. Recognize that taking care of yourself is crucial for your business's success, and don't feel guilty for prioritizing your well-being.

2. Start Small: If you're new to self-care practices, start small. Choose one or two activities that feel manageable and incorporate them into your daily routine. For example, commit to going for a 10-minute walk each morning or taking five minutes to practice deep breathing exercises.

3. Create a Routine: Establishing a routine can help make self-care practices feel more manageable and accessible. Choose a consistent time each day to engage in self-care activities, such as first thing in the morning or during a designated break in your workday.

4. Be Mindful: As you engage in self-care practices, be present and mindful. Focus on the sensations and experiences of the activity, and let go of any distracting thoughts or worries. Mindfulness can help you fully reap the benefits of self-care practices.

5. Get Creative: Self-care doesn't have to look a certain way. Get creative and find self-care activities that resonate with you. Some entrepreneurs find solace in artistic endeavors, such as painting or playing music. Others might find joy in cooking, gardening, or spending time with loved ones.

6. Don't Neglect Basic Needs: Basic needs such as sleep, nutrition, and hydration are essential components of self-care. Make sure you're getting enough sleep each night, eating a balanced and nutritious diet, and drinking plenty of water throughout the day.

7. Ask for Help: It's okay to ask for help in incorporating self-care practices into your daily routine. Consider enlisting the support of a coach, therapist, or trusted friend to hold you accountable and offer encouragement as you prioritize your well-being.

Incorporating self-care practices into your daily routine can be challenging, but it's essential for your overall well-being and success as an entrepreneur. By making self-care a priority, starting small, creating a routine, being mindful, getting creative, not neglecting basic needs, and asking for help, you can cultivate a more fulfilling and balanced life.

It's also important to practice self-compassion and forgiveness. Don't beat yourself up if you miss a day of self-care, and remember that self-care is an ongoing practice, not a one-time event.

Additional Tips for Self-Care and Wellness

In addition to incorporating self-care practices into your daily routine, there are several other tips for promoting wellness and self-care as an entrepreneur. Here are some additional tips:

1. Practice Mindfulness Meditation: Mindfulness meditation is a powerful tool for reducing stress and promoting well-being. It involves focusing your attention on the present moment and accepting it without judgment. Mindfulness meditation has been shown to improve mental health, reduce anxiety and depression, and increase overall well-being.

2. Take Breaks: As an entrepreneur, it can be easy to get caught up in your work and neglect taking breaks. However, taking regular breaks throughout the day can help you feel more energized,

focused, and productive. Schedule breaks into your workday, and use this time to engage in self-care activities or simply rest and recharge.

3. Prioritize Sleep: Sleep is essential for your physical and mental health. Make sure you're getting enough sleep each night, and prioritize creating a sleep-friendly environment. This might involve investing in a comfortable mattress and pillow, creating a relaxing bedtime routine, and limiting screen time before bed.

4. Move Your Body: Regular physical activity is crucial for overall well-being. Find ways to incorporate movement into your daily routine, whether that's through a morning yoga practice, a midday walk, or an evening workout. Exercise has been shown to reduce stress, improve mood, and boost energy levels.

5. Connect with Others: Connection with others is an essential component of well-being. As an entrepreneur, it can be easy to feel isolated and disconnected from others. Make an effort to connect with peers, colleagues, or loved ones regularly. This might involve attending networking events, scheduling coffee dates with colleagues, or simply reaching out to a friend for support.

6. Seek Professional Help: It's important to recognize when self-care practices aren't enough and to seek professional help when necessary Consider working with a therapist or coach who can provide support and guidance as you navigate the challenges of entrepreneurship.

Incorporating self-care practices into your daily routine and prioritizing your well-being is essential for success as an entrepreneur. By practicing mindfulness meditation, taking breaks, prioritizing sleep, moving your body, connecting with others, and seeking professional help when necessary, you can cultivate a more fulfilling and balanced life. Remember, taking care of yourself is crucial for your business's success, and you deserve to prioritize your well-being.

Conclusion

In this chapter, we've explored the importance of self-care and wellness practices for maintaining your energy, focus, and resilience as an entrepreneur. We've discussed the benefits of self-care, tips for incorporating self-care into your daily routine, and additional tips for maintaining your well-being.

Now, it's time to take action. Take a moment to reflect on your own self-care practices and well-being. Are there areas where you could prioritize self-care more effectively? How can you incorporate self-care into your daily routine in a way that works for you?

Remember, gorgeous, taking care of yourself is essential for achieving your goals and dreams as an entrepreneur. Prioritize self-care and wellness, and don't neglect your well-being in the pursuit of success. In the final chapter, we'll wrap up our journey together and reflect on the transformation you've undergone as a result of this book. Get ready to celebrate your growth and success, gorgeous, because you deserve it!

*"Self-care is giving the world the best of you,
instead of what's left of you."
— Katie Reed*

CHAPTER 15: CELEBRATING YOUR GROWTH AND SUCCESS

Welcome to chapter 15 of Think Big, Act Bold! In this chapter, we'll reflect on the transformation you've undergone as a result of this book, and celebrate your growth and success as an entrepreneur. You've come a long way, gorgeous, and it's time to acknowledge and celebrate your achievements.

In this chapter, we'll discuss the importance of celebrating your successes, and provide tips for setting and achieving new goals.

The Importance of Celebrating Your Successes

As an entrepreneur, it's easy to get caught up in the day-to-day struggles of running a business. There are always new challenges to face, goals to achieve, and obstacles to overcome. In the midst of all this, it can be easy to forget to celebrate your successes. However, taking the time to acknowledge and celebrate your achievements is essential for your mental health and overall well-being.

Celebrating your successes helps to build your confidence and self-esteem. When you take the time to recognize and acknowledge your achievements, you remind yourself of your capabilities and strengths. This can help you feel more confident in your abilities and more motivated to continue pursuing your goals.

Moreover, celebrating your successes can help to reduce stress and anxiety. Entrepreneurship is inherently stressful, and it's easy to get caught up in the day-to-day struggles. However, when you take the time to celebrate your successes, you're able to step back and see the bigger picture. You're able to recognize that all your hard work is paying off and that you're making progress towards your goals. This can help you feel more optimistic and less stressed about the challenges you're facing.

Celebrating your successes also helps you to stay motivated and focused. When you acknowledge and celebrate your achievements, you're able to see the progress you've made and the impact you're having. This can be incredibly motivating and can help you stay focused on your goals. Celebrating your successes can help you stay inspired and committed to your vision, even when faced with setbacks or challenges.

There are many ways to celebrate your successes as an entrepreneur. You might take a day off to relax and recharge, treat yourself to a special meal or activity, or simply take the time to reflect on your achievements and express gratitude for your progress. It's important to find a way to celebrate that feels meaningful and authentic to you.

In addition to celebrating your own successes, it's important to celebrate the successes of others as well. Recognizing the achievements of your colleagues, peers, and team members can help to build a sense of community and collaboration. Celebrating the successes of others can also inspire and motivate you to continue pursuing your own goals.

In conclusion, celebrating your successes is essential for your mental health, well-being, and success as an entrepreneur. By taking the time to acknowledge and celebrate your achievements, you can build your confidence and self-esteem, reduce stress and anxiety, and stay motivated and focused on your goals. Remember to celebrate your successes in a way that feels authentic and meaningful to you, and don't forget to celebrate the successes of others as well.

Tips for Setting and Achieving New Goals

Setting and achieving goals is a crucial aspect of personal and professional growth. When we set goals, we give ourselves direction and purpose. However, setting goals is not enough. We must also work towards achieving them. In this section, we will discuss tips for setting and achieving new goals.

1. Start with a clear vision: Before you can set goals, you need to have a clear vision of what you want to achieve. This vision should be specific, measurable, and achievable. For example, instead of setting a goal to "lose weight," set a goal to "lose 10 pounds in the next 3 months."

2. Write down your goals: Writing down your goals makes them more tangible and increases the likelihood that you will achieve them. Make sure your goals are SMART (specific, measurable, achievable, relevant, and time-bound).

3. Break your goals into smaller, manageable steps: When we set big goals, they can seem overwhelming and unattainable. Breaking them into smaller, manageable steps makes them more achievable and helps you to stay motivated.

4. Use positive affirmations: Positive affirmations are statements that you repeat to yourself to help you stay motivated and focused on your goals. Examples of positive affirmations include "I am capable of achieving my goals" and "I am worthy of success."

5. Stay accountable: Find someone who can hold you accountable for your goals. This could be a friend, family member, or coach. Share your goals with them and ask them to check in with you regularly to see how you are progressing.

6. Celebrate your progress: Celebrating your progress, no matter how small, helps to keep you motivated and focused on your goals. Set up rewards for yourself for reaching certain milestones along the way.

7. Stay flexible: Remember that sometimes things don't go according to plan. Stay flexible and willing to adjust your goals as needed. This doesn't mean giving up on them, but rather being open to new approaches and strategies.

8. Keep your goals visible: Place reminders of your goals in places where you will see them often. This could be a vision board, a sticky note on your computer, or a daily reminder on your phone.

9.   Practice self-compassion: Remember that setbacks and failures are a natural part of the goal-setting process. Practice self-compassion and be kind to yourself when things don't go according to plan. Use these setbacks as an opportunity to learn and grow.

By following these tips, you can set and achieve new goals with confidence and ease. Remember that setting and achieving goals is a process, and it takes time and effort. Be patient and persistent, and celebrate your successes along the way.

Celebrating Your Growth and Success

When you're on a journey to build a successful business and live your dream life, it's important to take a moment to reflect on your progress and celebrate your growth and success. Celebrating your wins can help you stay motivated, boost your confidence, and reinforce positive behaviors and habits that contribute to your success.

One of the most effective ways to celebrate your growth and success is to acknowledge and appreciate your progress. Take the time to reflect on your achievements, no matter how small they may seem. Celebrate every milestone, from landing a new client or hitting a revenue goal, to overcoming a personal challenge or learning a new skill. Celebrating your wins can help you stay focused on your goals and keep you motivated to keep moving forward.

Another way to celebrate your success is to share your wins with others. Whether it's through social media, your email newsletter, or in-person conversations, don't be afraid to share your accomplishments with your community. Celebrating your successes publicly can help you build credibility and attract new clients or customers, as well as inspire others to pursue their own dreams and goals.

In addition to acknowledging and sharing your wins, it's also important to take care of yourself and indulge in some self-care. Treat yourself to a massage, a night out with friends, or a relaxing weekend getaway. Celebrating your success should be a joyful and rewarding experience, so don't be afraid to splurge a little and do something special for yourself.

Finally, celebrating your growth and success is a great opportunity to set new goals and continue pushing yourself to achieve even more. Use your wins as motivation to set bigger and better goals for yourself and your business. Remember that success is a journey, not a destination, and there is always room for growth and improvement.

Overall, celebrating your growth and success is an essential part of building a successful and fulfilling life and business. Take the time to acknowledge and appreciate your progress, share your wins with others, indulge in some self-care, and set new goals for the future. With these practices, you'll be well on your way to achieving your dreams and living your best life.

*"I've learned that small achievements mean a lot,
and they should be celebrated.
Celebrating them helps you stay motivated
to keep working on the next small achievement,
which eventually leads to big achievements."*
— Cara Alwill Leyba

CHAPTER 16: ESSENTIAL HABITS AND PRACTICES FOR BOOSTING YOUR PRODUCTIVITY AND FOCUS

Welcome to Chapter 16 of Think Big, Act Bold! In this chapter, we'll explore essential habits and practices for boosting your productivity and focus as a woman entrepreneur. As an entrepreneur, your ability to manage your time and stay focused on your goals is crucial to your success.

In this chapter, we'll discuss the importance of prioritization, time management, and creating a supportive work environment.

Prioritization

One of the keys to boosting your productivity and focus is prioritization. Prioritization is a critical aspect of achieving success, both in business and in life. It involves identifying the most important tasks or goals and focusing your time and energy on those priorities. When you prioritize effectively, you can maximize your productivity, make progress towards your goals, and ultimately achieve greater success.

There are many different strategies for prioritizing, and the most effective approach will vary depending on your unique circumstances and goals. However, there are some general tips and best practices that can help you prioritize more effectively:

1. Set Clear Goals: Before you can prioritize effectively, you need to have a clear understanding of what you want to achieve. Take the time to define your goals in detail and write them down. This will help you stay focused and motivated as you work towards them.

2. Determine Urgency and Importance: One common prioritization framework is the Eisenhower Matrix, which involves categorizing tasks based on their urgency and importance. Urgent tasks require immediate attention, while important tasks contribute significantly to your long-term goals. By focusing on the tasks that are both urgent and important, you can make the most of your time and energy.

3. Focus on Your Most Important Tasks First: Once you have identified your most important tasks, focus your attention on them first. This can help you make significant progress towards your goals and avoid getting bogged down by less important tasks.

4. Break Tasks into Smaller Pieces: Large or complex tasks can be overwhelming, making it difficult to prioritize effectively. Breaking these tasks into smaller, more manageable pieces can help you make progress and stay motivated.

5. Eliminate Distractions: Distractions can derail even the most well-planned prioritization strategy. To stay focused, eliminate distractions such as social media notifications or email alerts when you are working on important tasks.

6. Re-Evaluate Regularly: Priorities can shift over time, so it's important to re-evaluate your priorities regularly. Take the time to assess your progress towards your goals and adjust your priorities as needed.

Prioritization is a key skill for achieving success, but it can be challenging to master. By setting clear goals, determining urgency and importance, focusing on important tasks first, breaking tasks into smaller pieces, eliminating distractions, and re-evaluating regularly, you can prioritize more effectively and achieve your goals with greater ease.

To prioritize effectively, start by creating a list of your tasks and activities for the day or week. Then, rank them in order of importance, based on their impact on your business goals. Focus your energy on the most important tasks first, and tackle the lower-priority tasks later in the day or week.

Time Management

Time is a precious commodity for any entrepreneur, and managing it effectively can be the difference between success and failure. As a business owner, you likely have multiple responsibilities to juggle on a daily basis, from managing your team and handling customer inquiries to marketing your business and keeping up with industry trends. To make the most of your time and avoid burnout, it's essential to prioritize your tasks and develop effective time management strategies.

One of the first steps in effective time management is understanding your priorities. Make a list of all the tasks and responsibilities you have, and then rank them in order of importance. This will help you identify the tasks that require your immediate attention and those that can be delegated or put on hold. It's also important to be realistic about how much time you have available for each task. Avoid overloading your schedule with too many commitments, as this can lead to stress and overwhelm.

Once you've established your priorities, it's time to develop a system for managing your time. One effective approach is to use a calendar or scheduling tool to plan out your days and weeks. This can help you stay on track with your goals and avoid wasting time on non-essential tasks. Consider using time-blocking techniques to set aside specific chunks of time for each task, and avoid multitasking as much as possible. Research has shown that multitasking can actually decrease productivity and lead to more errors.

Another important aspect of time management is learning how to delegate tasks to others. As a business owner, it can be tempting to try to do everything yourself. However, this is not always the most efficient or effective approach. Identify the tasks that can be outsourced or delegated to team members, and then communicate your expectations clearly. This will not only free up your time but also empower your team and help them develop their own skills and expertise.

In addition to delegating tasks, it's also important to take breaks and prioritize self-care. This may seem counterintuitive, but research has shown that taking regular breaks can actually improve productivity and help prevent burnout. Set aside time each day to engage in activities that you enjoy, whether it's taking a walk outside, practicing meditation, or spending time with loved ones. This can help you recharge your batteries and return to your work with renewed energy and focus.

Finally, remember that time management is an ongoing process. What works for you today may not work for you tomorrow, as your business and personal responsibilities evolve. Be open to trying new techniques and strategies, and regularly evaluate your progress to identify areas for improvement. By staying organized, prioritizing your tasks, and practicing effective time management, you can achieve your goals and build a successful business without sacrificing your health and well-being.

Creating a Supportive Work Environment

As a woman entrepreneur, you have the power to create a work environment that not only benefits your business but also fosters a positive and healthy workplace culture. This means taking into consideration the physical and emotional well-being of yourself and your team members.

Here are some key factors to consider when creating a supportive work environment:

1. Physical Space: Your workspace should be designed in a way that promotes productivity, creativity, and comfort. It should be well-lit, well-ventilated, and free from clutter. Invest in ergonomic chairs, desks, and other equipment to help reduce physical strain and promote good posture.

2. Flexibility: Providing flexible work options such as remote work, flexible hours, or job sharing can be a huge benefit to employees. It helps them balance their work and personal lives and can lead to increased job satisfaction and productivity.

3. Open Communication: Create an open and transparent communication policy that encourages employees to share their

thoughts, concerns, and feedback. This helps build trust and a sense of community in the workplace.

4. Empowerment: Empower your team members by delegating tasks, providing them with the resources and training they need to succeed, and recognizing their achievements. This helps build confidence, trust, and loyalty among employees.

5. Diversity and Inclusion: Encourage diversity and inclusivity in the workplace by creating a safe and welcoming environment for employees of all backgrounds. This includes offering equal opportunities for career advancement and providing training on diversity, equity, and inclusion.

6. Work-Life Balance: Encourage a healthy work-life balance by promoting self-care, providing mental health resources, and offering paid time off. This helps employees feel valued and supported, leading to higher job satisfaction and productivity.

Creating a supportive work environment takes effort and time, but the benefits are immense. Not only will it increase productivity and job satisfaction, but it will also help attract and retain top talent. As a woman entrepreneur, it's important to lead by example and prioritize the well-being of yourself and your team members.

Conclusion

In this chapter, we've explored essential habits and practices for boosting your productivity and focus as a woman entrepreneur. We've discussed the importance of prioritization, time management, and creating a supportive work environment.

Now, it's time to take action. Take a moment to reflect on your own productivity and focus habits and practices. Are there areas where you could improve your prioritization or time management skills? How can you create a more supportive work environment that allows you to thrive as an entrepreneur?

Remember, gorgeous, your productivity and focus are essential to your success as an entrepreneur. Keep refining your habits and practices, and don't be afraid to experiment and try new things. In the next chapter, we'll explore how to create a clear and compelling vision for your business and life, so get ready to dream big and think boldly!

*"Productivity is not just about doing more.
It is about creating more impact with less work."*
— Prerna Malik

CHAPTER 17: HOW TO CREATE A CLEAR AND COMPELLING VISION FOR YOUR BUSINESS AND LIFE

Welcome to Chapter 17 of Think Big, Act Bold! In this chapter, we'll explore how to create a clear and compelling vision for your business and life. As a woman entrepreneur, having a clear and inspiring vision is essential for staying focused and motivated on your entrepreneurial journey.

In this chapter, we'll discuss the importance of having a vision, how to create a vision that aligns with your values and goals, and how to stay motivated and focused on your vision.

The Importance of Having a Vision

Having a vision is crucial for success in any area of life, and especially in entrepreneurship. Without a clear and compelling vision, it is easy to get lost in the day-to-day tasks and lose sight of the bigger picture. Your vision is what gives you direction and purpose, and it helps you stay focused and motivated even when faced with challenges and setbacks.

So, what exactly is a vision? In simple terms, it is a clear and inspiring picture of what you want to achieve in your life or business. It is a description of your ideal future, and it reflects your deepest values, passions, and aspirations. Your vision should be something that excites and energizes you, and it should be something that you are truly committed to achieving.

Having a vision is important for several reasons. First and foremost, it gives you a sense of direction and purpose. When you have a clear vision, you know exactly what you are working towards, and you can make decisions and take actions that are aligned with that vision. This helps you stay focused and motivated, and it makes it easier to prioritize your time and resources.

Secondly, having a vision helps you overcome obstacles and challenges. When you are faced with a difficult situation, it can be easy to lose sight of your goals and get bogged down in the details. However, if you have a clear vision in mind, you can use it as a source of inspiration and motivation to push through the tough times.

Finally, having a vision helps you attract the right people and resources to your business. When you have a compelling vision that resonates with others, it makes it easier to build a team of like-minded individuals who share your values and are committed to achieving the same goals. It also makes it easier to attract customers and partners who believe in your vision and want to support your mission.

So, how do you create a vision for your life or business? The first step is to spend some time reflecting on your values, passions, and aspirations. Ask yourself what is most important to you, and what you want to achieve in the long term. Think about what kind of impact you want to have on the world, and what legacy you want to leave behind.

Once you have a clear understanding of your values and aspirations, you can start to create a vision statement. A vision statement is a concise and inspiring description of your ideal future. It should be written in the present tense, as if you have already achieved your goals, and it should be specific and measurable.

For example, if your vision is to create a successful and sustainable business, your vision statement might look something like this: "We are a thriving and innovative business that is making a positive impact on our customers, employees, and the world. We are known for our high-quality products, exceptional customer service, and commitment to sustainability."

Once you have created your vision statement, it is important to keep it front and center in your mind at all times. Post it somewhere visible, such as on your computer or phone, and read it every day to remind yourself of what you are working towards. Use it as a guidepost to help you make decisions and take actions that are aligned with your vision.

In conclusion, having a clear and compelling vision is essential for success in life and business. It gives you direction and purpose, helps you overcome obstacles, and attracts the right people and resources to your mission. By taking the time to create a vision statement that reflects your values and aspirations, you can stay focused and motivated on your path to success.

Creating a Vision that Aligns with Your Values and Goals

Creating a clear and compelling vision for your life and business is essential for achieving success. Without a vision, you may find yourself wandering aimlessly, unsure of what you truly want to achieve or how to get there. A powerful vision serves as a beacon, guiding your actions and decisions toward your desired destination.

When creating your vision, it is important to consider your core values and goals. What drives you? What is most important to you? What do you want to achieve? Take time to reflect on these questions and write down your answers. This will serve as the foundation for your vision.

Your vision should be ambitious, yet realistic. It should stretch you out of your comfort zone, but also be achievable with hard work and dedication. It should be specific, so that you know exactly what you are working toward. And it should be motivating and inspiring, so that it energizes you and keeps you focused on your goals.

To create a vision that aligns with your values and goals, consider the following steps:

1. Reflect on your values and goals: Take some time to reflect on what is most important to you and what you want to achieve. Write down your core values and long-term goals, and consider how they can be integrated into your vision.

2. Visualize your ideal future: Imagine yourself in the future, living your ideal life and running a successful business. What does it look like? What does it feel like? Use this visualization to create a clear picture of your desired outcome.

3. Create a vision statement: Use the insights from your reflection and visualization to create a clear and concise vision statement. This statement should capture the essence of your desired future and serve as a guidepost for your actions and decisions.

4. Break down your vision into actionable steps: Once you have a clear vision, break it down into specific, measurable, and actionable steps. This will help you to create a roadmap for achieving your vision and ensure that you are making progress toward your goals.

5. Review and adjust your vision regularly: Your vision should be a living document that evolves with you over time. Review your vision regularly and adjust it as needed to ensure that it remains aligned with your values and goals.

By creating a clear and compelling vision for your life and business, you can stay focused on your goals and achieve greater success. Remember to be ambitious, yet realistic, and to use your vision as a guidepost for your actions and decisions. With hard work, dedication, and a clear vision, you can achieve anything you set your mind to.

To create a vision that aligns with your values and goals, start by reflecting on your core values and beliefs, and the impact you want to make on the world. Then, identify your long-term goals and aspirations, and create a vision statement that reflects your purpose and vision for your business and life.

Staying Motivated and Focused on Your Vision

Having a clear vision is essential for success, but it's not enough to just create a vision and then forget about it. To achieve your goals and make your vision a reality, you need to stay motivated and focused on it.

One way to stay motivated is to remind yourself of the reasons why you started on this journey in the first place. Think about what inspired you to become an entrepreneur and what you hope to achieve. Write down your goals and the steps you need to take to achieve them. Break down your goals into smaller, more manageable tasks, and track your progress along the way.

Another way to stay motivated is to surround yourself with positive influences. Connect with like-minded individuals who share your values and goals. Attend events, join groups or clubs, and network with others in your industry. These connections can provide support, advice, and motivation when you need it most.

It's also important to take care of yourself physically, mentally, and emotionally. Get enough rest, eat a healthy diet, and exercise regularly. Take time to relax and engage in activities that bring you joy and fulfillment. When you feel good about yourself, you're more likely to stay motivated and focused on your vision.

Remember that setbacks and challenges are a natural part of the journey to success. Don't let them discourage you or derail your progress. Instead, use them as opportunities to learn and grow. Reflect on what went wrong, and consider how you can approach the situation differently in the future. Seek advice and support from your network and mentors, and don't be afraid to ask for help when you need it.

Finally, celebrate your successes along the way. Recognize your accomplishments, no matter how small they may seem. Take time to appreciate your hard work and the progress you've made. Celebrating your successes can provide the motivation and inspiration you need to keep pushing forward and stay focused on your vision.

Conclusion

In this chapter, we've explored how to create a clear and compelling vision for your business and life. We've discussed the importance of having a vision, how to create a vision that aligns with your values and goals, and how to stay motivated and focused on your vision.

Remember, gorgeous, your vision is essential for staying focused and motivated on your entrepreneurial journey. Keep refining and revisiting your vision, and don't be afraid to make adjustments as you grow and evolve as an entrepreneur.

In the next chapter, we'll explore the power of goal setting and action planning for achieving your dreams. Get ready to set some bold and exciting goals, and take action towards your vision and goals!

"The only thing worse than being blind
is having sight but no vision."
— Helen Keller

CHAPTER 18: THE POWER OF GOAL SETTING AND ACTION PLANNING FOR ACHIEVING YOUR DREAMS

Welcome to Chapter 18 of Think Big, Act Bold! In this chapter, we'll explore the power of goal setting and action planning for achieving your dreams. As a woman entrepreneur, setting clear and ambitious goals is essential for staying focused, motivated, and on track towards your vision.

In this chapter, we'll discuss how to set effective goals, how to create an action plan to achieve your goals, and how to stay motivated and accountable along the way.

Setting Effective Goals

Setting goals is an important part of achieving success in business and in life. Goals help you to create a clear roadmap for where you want to go and what you want to achieve. They help you to stay focused and motivated, and they give you something to work towards. However, setting effective goals is not always easy. In this section, we will explore the key steps to setting effective goals that will help you to achieve success.

Step 1: Identify Your Goals

The first step to setting effective goals is to identify what you want to achieve. This involves taking the time to think about what is important to you and what you want to accomplish in your life and business. This might include both short-term and long-term goals. Short-term goals might include things like launching a new product, while long-term goals might include things like growing your business to a certain level or achieving a specific income goal.

To identify your goals, it can be helpful to use a brainstorming technique. Take some time to write down all of the things that you want to accomplish. Don't worry about whether or not they are achievable or realistic at this stage - just focus on getting your ideas down on paper.

Step 2: Make Your Goals Specific and Measurable

Once you have identified your goals, the next step is to make them specific and measurable. This means that you need to define exactly what you want to achieve and how you will measure your progress. For example, instead of setting a goal to "grow your business," you might set a goal to "increase your monthly revenue by 20% over the next 6 months."

Making your goals specific and measurable helps you to stay focused and motivated because you have a clear target to work towards. It also makes it easier to track your progress and adjust your strategies if necessary.

Step 3: Break Your Goals Down into Actionable Steps

Setting a goal is just the first step. To achieve your goals, you need to break them down into actionable steps. This means identifying the specific actions you need to take to move closer to your goals. For example, if your goal is to increase your monthly revenue by 20% over the next 6 months, your actionable steps might include things like:

- Researching and implementing new marketing strategies
- Launching a new product or service
- Reaching out to potential new clients or customers
- Streamlining your business processes to increase efficiency

Breaking your goals down into actionable steps makes them more manageable and less overwhelming. It also helps you to stay on track and make progress towards your goals.

Step 4: Set Realistic Timelines

Setting realistic timelines is an important part of setting effective goals. This means giving yourself enough time to achieve your goals while also making sure that your timelines are challenging enough to keep you motivated. To set realistic timelines, it can be helpful to break your goals down into smaller, more manageable steps and then assign deadlines to each step.

It's also important to be flexible with your timelines. Sometimes things take longer than expected, and that's okay. The key is to keep moving forward and making progress towards your goals, even if it takes a little longer than you originally anticipated.

Step 5: Hold Yourself Accountable

Setting goals is only the first step. To achieve your goals, you need to hold yourself accountable. This means taking responsibility for your actions and making sure that you are making progress towards your goals. One way to hold yourself accountable is to track your progress and review your goals regularly. This can help you to identify any areas where you may be falling behind and make adjustments to your strategies if necessary.

Another way to hold yourself accountable is to share your goals with others. This can be a powerful motivator because it creates a sense of social pressure to achieve your goals. When you share your goals with others, they become invested in your success and may offer support or hold you accountable. This can be especially helpful when you encounter obstacles or setbacks along the way.

Knowing that others are counting on you can be a powerful motivator to keep pushing forward and stay focused on your goals. Additionally, sharing your goals with others can open up new opportunities or connections that can help you achieve them. For example, if you share your goal of starting a new business with a friend, they may know someone who can offer guidance or support in getting started.

However, it's important to choose the right people to share your goals with. You want to find individuals who are supportive and encouraging, rather than those who may be critical or dismissive of your aspirations. It's also important to remember that ultimately, your goals are for you and you alone. While outside support can be helpful, your motivation and determination should come from within.

In addition to sharing your goals with others, it can also be helpful to track your progress and celebrate small wins along the way. This not only helps you stay motivated and focused, but it also allows you to see how far you've come and feel a sense of pride in your accomplishments. When setting goals, it's important to break them down into smaller, more manageable tasks and set specific deadlines for each one. This not only makes your goals more achievable, but it also helps you stay on track and monitor your progress.

Finally, it's important to be flexible and adaptable when it comes to your goals. Life is unpredictable and there may be unexpected obstacles or opportunities that arise along the way. It's important to be open to adjusting your goals and plans as needed, while still staying focused on your overall vision and values. With the right mindset, strategies, and support, setting and achieving effective goals can be a powerful tool for creating the life and business you truly desire.

Creating an Action Plan

Creating an action plan is a crucial step towards achieving your goals. Once you have set clear, achievable goals, it's important to map out the steps you need to take to reach them. An action plan is essentially a roadmap that outlines the specific tasks, timelines, and resources required to achieve your goals.

To begin creating your action plan, break down your goals into smaller, more manageable tasks. This will help you avoid feeling overwhelmed by the big picture and give you a clear idea of what needs to be done. Determine what steps you need to take to complete each task and assign a deadline to each one. This will help you stay on track and hold yourself accountable for completing each step.

In addition to breaking down your goals into smaller tasks, it's important to consider the resources you will need to achieve them. This might include financial resources, time, and access to expertise or technology. Identify what resources you need and make a plan to acquire them.

When creating your action plan, it's also helpful to anticipate potential obstacles that may arise and have a plan in place to address them. This will help you avoid getting derailed when unexpected challenges arise.

Regularly reviewing and revising your action plan is also important. As you progress towards your goals, you may encounter new information or obstacles that require adjustments to your plan. By regularly reviewing and revising your action plan, you can stay on track and ensure that you are taking the necessary steps to achieve your goals.

In addition to creating an action plan for each of your goals, it can be helpful to prioritize your goals and determine which ones require immediate attention. By prioritizing your goals, you can focus your energy and resources on the most important tasks, rather than spreading yourself too thin.

Remember, creating an action plan is just the first step towards achieving your goals. The real work begins when you start taking action and working towards your goals. But with a clear plan in place, you will be better equipped to stay focused, overcome obstacles, and ultimately achieve the success you desire.

Staying Motivated and Accountable

Staying motivated and accountable is a crucial component of achieving your goals. It's easy to start out with enthusiasm, but as time goes on, it can become challenging to maintain the same level of energy and commitment. That's why it's essential to have strategies in place to stay motivated and hold yourself accountable.

One effective way to stay motivated is to keep reminding yourself of why you set the goal in the first place. What was the driving force behind your decision to pursue this goal? What will you gain from achieving it? Reflecting on these questions regularly can help reignite your motivation and keep you focused on the end result.

Another strategy for staying motivated is to break your goal down into smaller, more manageable steps. This approach makes it easier to see progress and helps prevent you from becoming overwhelmed. Celebrating small victories along the way can also boost your motivation and provide a sense of accomplishment.

Accountability is also critical for goal achievement. It's easy to let yourself off the hook when you're the only one holding yourself accountable. That's why it's beneficial to have someone to whom you can be accountable. This can be a friend, mentor, or coach who checks in with you regularly to ensure you're making progress toward your goal.

Additionally, setting deadlines and tracking your progress can help you stay accountable. Make a plan for what you'll accomplish each week or month, and track your progress toward those milestones. Seeing your progress on paper can be a powerful motivator to keep going.

Finally, it's essential to be kind to yourself throughout the process. Setbacks and challenges are a natural part of the journey, and beating yourself up over them will only sap your motivation. Instead, practice self-compassion and remind yourself that setbacks are opportunities for growth and learning.

By staying motivated and accountable, you'll be much more likely to achieve your goals and live the life you envision for yourself.

To stay accountable, seek out support and feedback from a mentor, peer, or advisor. Share your goals and action plan with someone who can provide guidance, encouragement, and accountability as you work towards achieving your goals.

Conclusion

In this chapter, we've explored the power of goal setting and action planning for achieving your dreams. We've discussed how to set effective goals, create an action plan, and stay motivated and accountable along the way.

Remember, gorgeous, setting clear and ambitious goals is essential for achieving your vision and making your entrepreneurial dreams a reality. Keep refining and revisiting your goals and action plan, and don't be afraid to adjust your plan as you grow and evolve as an entrepreneur.

In the next chapter, we'll explore how to overcome common challenges in business and life with resilience and grace. Get ready to build your resilience muscles, and stay strong and focused on your entrepreneurial journey!

*"By recording your dreams and goals on paper,
you set in motion the process of becoming
the person you most want to be. Put your future in
good hands — your own."*
— Mark Victor Hansen

CHAPTER 19: OVERCOMING COMMON CHALLENGES IN BUSINESS AND LIFE WITH RESILIENCE AND GRACE

Welcome to Chapter 19 of Think Big, Act Bold! In this chapter, we'll explore the importance of developing resilience and grace in the face of common challenges in business and life. As a woman entrepreneur, you're likely to face many obstacles and setbacks on your journey to success. But with resilience and grace, you can overcome these challenges and emerge stronger than ever.

In this chapter, we'll discuss common challenges women entrepreneurs face, strategies for building resilience and grace, and real-life examples of women who have overcome challenges with resilience and grace.

Common Challenges Women Entrepreneurs Face

Women entrepreneurs face a variety of challenges that can hinder their success. Some of these challenges include gender bias, lack of access to funding and resources, and the need to balance work and family responsibilities. These challenges can be discouraging, but it is important to remember that they can be overcome.

One of the most common challenges faced by women entrepreneurs is gender bias. Women are often subject to stereotypes and biases that can affect their ability to succeed in business. For example, women are often perceived as being less capable or less committed to their work than men. This bias can manifest in a number of ways, such as a lack of respect from colleagues or investors, or being passed over for opportunities.

Another challenge that women entrepreneurs face is a lack of access to funding and resources. Women-owned businesses receive less funding than businesses owned by men, despite the fact that women are starting businesses at a faster rate than men. This can make it difficult for women to get their businesses off the ground or to scale their operations.

The need to balance work and family responsibilities is also a significant challenge for many women entrepreneurs. Women are more likely than men to take on primary caregiving responsibilities for children and elderly family members, which can limit their ability to focus on their businesses. This can be especially challenging for women who are starting their businesses while also raising young children.

Women entrepreneurs face a wide range of challenges, both in business and in life. These may include:

- Financial challenges: Many women entrepreneurs struggle to secure funding or investment for their businesses, or to manage cash flow effectively.
- Work-life balance: Balancing the demands of running a business with family and personal responsibilities can be challenging for women entrepreneurs.
- Imposter syndrome: Many women struggle with imposter syndrome, feeling like they don't belong or aren't qualified to succeed as entrepreneurs.
- Discrimination: Women entrepreneurs may face discrimination based on their gender, race, ethnicity, or other factors.
- Burnout: Running a business can be demanding and stressful, and many women entrepreneurs struggle with burnout or exhaustion.

Despite these challenges, there are many successful women entrepreneurs who have overcome these obstacles and built thriving businesses. One key to success is to build a supportive network of mentors, peers, and advisors who can help you navigate the challenges of entrepreneurship. It is also important to stay focused on your vision and to be persistent in pursuing your goals. With hard work, determination, and a willingness to adapt and learn, women entrepreneurs can overcome the challenges they face and achieve great success.

Strategies for Building Resilience and Grace

Building resilience and grace can help women entrepreneurs overcome these challenges and emerge stronger and more successful. Here are some strategies for building resilience and grace:

- Practice self-care: Taking care of your physical, emotional, and mental health is essential for building resilience and grace. This may include regular exercise, healthy eating, meditation, or therapy.
- Cultivate a growth mindset: Embracing a growth mindset, which emphasizes learning, growth, and improvement, can help you overcome setbacks and challenges with resilience and grace.
- Seek support: Building a supportive network of mentors, peers, and advisors can help you navigate the challenges of entrepreneurship with resilience and grace.
- Embrace failure: Viewing failure as an opportunity for learning and growth, rather than as a personal failure, can help you bounce back from setbacks and challenges with resilience and grace.
- Practice gratitude: Cultivating a mindset of gratitude, and focusing on the positive aspects of your life and business, can help you maintain perspective and build resilience and grace.

Real-Life Examples of Resilience and Grace

While building resilience and grace can be challenging, there are many successful women entrepreneurs who have mastered the art of bouncing back from setbacks and facing challenges with poise and grace. Here are a few examples:

1. Sara Blakely: The founder of Spanx faced numerous rejections before finally finding success with her product. Blakely's resilience and positive mindset helped her stay focused and motivated, even in the face of rejection.

2.   Oprah Winfrey: Oprah Winfrey is a prime example of a woman who has faced adversity and come out on top. Despite growing up in poverty and facing numerous challenges throughout her life and career, Oprah has always stayed focused on her goals and remained resilient in the face of obstacles.

3.   Arianna Huffington: Arianna Huffington is the founder of the Huffington Post and is known for her resilience and ability to bounce back from setbacks. After collapsing from exhaustion in 2007, Huffington shifted her focus to self-care and prioritizing her health, which allowed her to come back even stronger.

4.   Mary Kay Ash: Mary Kay Ash founded Mary Kay Cosmetics at the age of 45 and went on to build a successful business empire. Despite facing numerous setbacks and challenges along the way, Ash's positive attitude and determination helped her stay focused on her goals and build a successful business.

5.   J.K. Rowling: J.K. Rowling, the author of the Harry Potter series, faced numerous rejections before finally finding a publisher for her books. Despite facing financial struggles and personal setbacks, Rowling's resilience and determination helped her persevere and become one of the most successful authors of all time.

These women serve as inspiration for anyone facing challenges in their personal or professional lives. By staying resilient, focused, and positive, it's possible to overcome even the toughest obstacles and achieve your dreams.

Conclusion

In this chapter, we've explored the importance of developing resilience and grace in the face of common challenges in business and life. We've discussed common challenges women entrepreneurs face, strategies for building resilience and grace, and real-life examples of women who have overcome challenges with resilience and grace.

We have many women that can serve as inspiration for us to continue to pursue our dreams and turn our passion into profits. And we can continue to be an inspiration to women of our future!

Remember, gorgeous, building resilience and grace takes time and effort, but it's essential for overcoming obstacles and achieving success as a woman entrepreneur. Keep practicing self-care, cultivating a growth mindset, seeking support, embracing failure, and practicing gratitude, and you'll be well on your way to a life of resilience and grace.

"You may encounter many defeats,
but you must not be defeated.
In fact, it may be necessary to encounter the defeats,
so you can know who you are,
what you can rise from,
how you can still come out of it."
— Maya Angelou

CONCLUSION: KEEP THINKING BIG, ACTING BOLD, AND SHINING BRIGHT

Congratulations! You've made it to the end of this book, and hopefully, you're feeling inspired and motivated to take action toward building the life and business of your dreams.

Remember, gorgeous, you are capable of achieving greatness. I want to leave you with some final words of encouragement and support. Being an entrepreneur is not easy, but it is one of the most rewarding and fulfilling journeys you can embark on. You have the skills, knowledge, and passion to create a business that aligns with your values and vision, and makes a positive impact on the world.

But before you close this book and move on to your next task, I want to leave you with some final thoughts and action steps.

Throughout this book, we've covered a lot of ground, from defining your dream life and business to cultivating resilience and perseverance. We've discussed the importance of setting big goals, cultivating a positive mindset, taking bold action, and staying true to your authentic self. We've also explored the power of gratitude, abundance, setting boundaries, and making a positive impact through your business. We've explored strategies for overcoming fear, self-doubt, and limiting beliefs, and we've discussed the importance of building a strong network of mentors, peers, and advisors. We've also delved into marketing and branding best practices, self-care and wellness, and goal setting and prioritization.

Now, it's time to take action. Take a moment to reflect on your growth and success, and set new goals that align with your vision and values. Remember to celebrate your successes along the way, and stay focused and dedicated to your entrepreneurial journey.

All of this information is useless if you don't take action on it. So, here are some steps you can take to turn the insights and ideas in this book into real-world results:

1. Define Your Dream Life and Business: If you haven't already, take some time to define your dream life and business. What do you want to achieve? What does success look like to you? Write down your goals and aspirations, and be as specific as possible. Then, break those goals down into smaller, more manageable steps that you can take action on.

2. Build Your Resilience Muscle: Building resilience takes time and practice. Start by identifying your limiting beliefs and self-doubt triggers. Then, work on reframing those thoughts and developing a growth mindset. Take small risks and celebrate your successes along the way. Remember, failure is not the opposite of success, but rather a part of the journey.

3. Build Your Support Network: Seek out mentors and advisors who can guide you on your journey. Attend networking events and seek out like-minded peers who can support and encourage you. Join online communities or mastermind groups to connect with other entrepreneurs who are on a similar path.

4. Embrace Marketing and Branding: Take time to develop a strong brand story that aligns with your values and goals. Use social media and content marketing to build your brand and connect with your audience. Stay up-to-date on marketing and branding best practices and be willing to experiment and pivot when necessary.

5. Prioritize Self-Care and Wellness: Make time for self-care practices that nurture your physical, mental, and emotional well-being. This includes things like exercise, meditation, and spending time in nature. Set boundaries and make time for rest and relaxation.

6. Celebrate Your Successes: Take time to celebrate your wins, no matter how small they may seem. Recognize your progress and use it as motivation to keep moving forward. Share your successes with your support network, and be proud of what you've achieved.

7. Take Action: Finally, take action on the insights and ideas in this book. Don't let fear or self-doubt hold you back. Remember, taking imperfect action is better than taking no action at all. Take the first step today and keep moving forward.

Building a successful life and business takes time, effort, and perseverance. But by cultivating resilience and grace, developing a positive mindset, building a supportive network, and taking action, you can turn your dreams into reality. In the face of challenges and setbacks, remember to stay resilient and focused on your goals. Surround yourself with positive and supportive people who believe in you and your vision, and never give up on yourself. So, go out there and make it happen!

Thank you for joining me on this journey, gorgeous. I am honored to have been your guide, and I can't wait to see the incredible things you will achieve as an entrepreneur. Keep thinking big, acting bold, and shining bright!

TAKE SOME TIME TO WRITE OUT SOME GOALS!

Writing out your goals will help you remember them and now you will have somewhere to come back to so you can check in on your progress.

WRITE OUT AT LEAST 10 AFFIRMATIONS

Come back when you are feeling "less than" so you can remind yourself of just how incredible you are! YOU GOT THIS!

SHOW SOME GRATITUDE

What are three things right now that you are grateful for? Recognizing what we are grateful for will help us appreciate more.

GIVE SOME ADVICE TO YOUR YOUNGER SELF

Remember all the things you worried about as a child? With all that you've experienced what advice would you give to your younger self now?

COME CONNECT WITH ME!!

Website: iammeganewing.com

YouTube: @iammeganewing

Instagram: @i_am_meganewing

Facebook: IamMeganEwing

ABOUT THE AUTHOR

Meet Megan, a passionate entrepreneur, motivational speaker, and all-around fun-loving woman! Megan's journey began when she left her corporate job to pursue her dream of starting her own business. After years of hard work, dedication, and a little bit of luck, she now runs a successful company and is determined to inspire others to do the same!

Megan is a successful entrepreneur, speaker, and coach who has dedicated her career to empowering women to pursue their dreams and achieve success on their own terms. With over 10 years of experience in entrepreneurship, she has a wealth of knowledge and expertise to share with her clients and readers.

Throughout her career, Megan has overcome numerous challenges and obstacles on her path to success. She understands firsthand the importance of resilience, perseverance, and a positive mindset, and she is passionate about helping others cultivate these traits in themselves.

As a coach and mentor, Megan is known for her compassionate and empowering approach. She believes that everyone has the potential to achieve their goals and live their dream life, and she is committed to helping her clients tap into that potential and create lasting success.

When she's not busy running her business or working with clients, Megan loves to travel, try new foods, and spend time with her husband and kids. Her mission is to empower women to live their best lives, both in business and in their personal lives. Through her writing Megan shares her own experiences and practical advice to help women overcome their fears and achieve their wildest dreams.

Join Megan on her journey to success, and discover how you too can create a life and business you love!